BEHIND
THE
GRANITE
WALLS

First, I want to dedicate this book to a couple of my oldest friends who are, in many ways, like long-distance family – **Christy and John**. I have known them for close to 30 years. Though we live nearly half a world away, we still know how important we are to each other.

Then there are newer friends who I have gotten to know since getting out, who have helped me adjust – **Jim, Cathy and Tash**.

And all those on the Isle of Man who welcomed me home, especially **Priscilla, Peter and Sarah, Lula and Glenn**. Your help has been most appreciated and welcomed.

BEHIND THE GRANITE WALLS

Back Inside America's Toughest Prisons

JAMIE MORGAN KANE

MIRROR BOOKS

MIRROR BOOKS

© Jamie Morgan Kane

The rights of Jamie Morgan Kane to be identified as the author
of this book have been asserted, in accordance with the
Copyright, Designs and Patents Act 1988.

1

Published in Great Britain and Ireland in 2022 by
Mirror Books, a Reach PLC business.

www.mirrorbooks.co.uk
@TheMirrorBooks

Print ISBN: 9781913406493
eBook ISBN: 9781913406516

Edited by Roy Gilfoyle, Richard Williamson and Laura McConville
Typeset by Adam Oldfield

Printed and bound in Great Britain by
CPI Group (UK) Ltd, Croydon, CR0 4YY

A CIP catalogue record for this book is available from the British Library.

Every effort has been made to fulfil requirements with regard to
reproducing copyright material. The author and publisher will be
glad to rectify any omissions at the earliest opportunity.

1 3 5 7 9 10 8 6 4 2

Cover image: iStock

CONTENTS

INTRODUCTION

In my first book, *34 Years in Hell*, I told the story of my life. After being born on the Isle of Man, I was taken to Canada as a baby and then transported into the United States of America. At the age of 14, I was sold to an American couple to replace, as I found out many years later, a child they had previously adopted who had mysteriously disappeared. I recounted how I had joined the US military the day I left school, in the belief that I was an American citizen. Circumstances later persuaded me to plead guilty to a crime I did not commit – having come home to find a corpse in the living room of my young family's home – and this resulted in me spending more than three decades in prison.

What is the 'Hell' that I wrote of? It comes in many forms to different people, but for me, it was the gradual loss of what little family and friends I had, through either death or drifting away from each other over the years. Then I found that I had to deal with district attorneys who did not keep the promises they had made in exchange for my guilty plea, incompetent state attorneys who failed me at every parole hearing, and prison officials who could not care less about what was right, as long as they could keep the bunks filled and themselves in a job.

I also had to deal with the Californian State law that was passed retrospectively, which kept those of us already serving our sentences in prison for even longer, as well as other inmates, who were happier in prison than out of it, spreading their own misery to all that they could.

Then came the real 'Hell' of finding out that my entire life had been lived as a lie, that I was not the person I thought I was, the mother I thought I knew was not related to me and, that instead of being an American citizen by adoption, I was instead what they called a 'Stateless Alien'. I wrote of my struggles to get out of prison and away from a country where I did not belong, to return home to one that had no memory of me. And as I had left when I was six months old, I had no memory of it either. Additionally, I was to learn that all of my immediate family had either passed away, would not acknowledge the fact I existed or didn't want to know me, so my questions about my history would never be answered.

Lastly, there came a day in 2013 when I went before a parole board and, wonder of wonders, parole was granted. However, in California, as in many US States, the state governor has a lengthy period in which he can override the parole board's decisions. Just two days before the end of this period, that is exactly what he did to me. When I asked why, I was told his answer was, 'Because I can!' With one stroke of his pen, he cost me another five years of freedom.

*****

Since my book was published, I have been asked, 'But what was prison really like?' This book attempts to answer that question. Prison is a word which conjures up different things to the people who hear it. To some, it is a place where people are simply locked away from society for a period of time. Others may think it is a place where torture, fear, violence and hopelessness are commonplace. Some might think it is a place of rehabilitation. Then there are those who believe it is a state of mind. Of course, I can only talk about the United States and the Californian prison system. But, having served 34½ years in their custody, I can honestly say it is all of the above… and more. The thing to remember about the system in the US is that prisons fall into three categories. First there are the county jails where, guilty or innocent, you are sent if you are arrested and held in custody – and where you serve your sentence if it is less than a couple of years. Next are the state prisons. Each state has its own 'Department of Corrections,' presumably so named as they are supposed to correct your behaviour. Most state prison websites have an inmate search facility, so anyone can see who is imprisoned – some states quite literally as they also post photos of their inmates, which they update yearly! Finally, there are the federal prisons, which hold inter-state prisoners.

So come with me, as I take you through the things that those in prison go through in their day-to-day existence, the hustles they get up to in order to survive, the people they find themselves forced to live with, and some of the prisons I have experienced.

Chapter 1

THE END OF LIFE AS YOU KNOW IT

First, let me begin by explaining what happens after you have been arrested and are awaiting trial in an American jail (gaol). From the moment the handcuffs are snapped on your wrists, your life will never be the same. I found it amazing, having spoken with hundreds, if not thousands of men, that the one thing they all said is that at the moment of arrest, they experienced their widest range of emotions. Usually, it starts with the disbelief that they were caught, followed by a flood of thoughts on how they were going to beat this. You may find it funny, but many actually try to convince themselves that they didn't do it, or that someone snitched on them, or even that the cops had set them up.

When you arrive at the jail, whether by patrol car or a paddy wagon, the next step is always the same. You will

5

be taken to a booking area and have everything taken from your pockets, as well as your belt and shoestrings (because people have been known to use them to hang themselves, which really upsets the staff), which is all inventoried and placed in an envelope. It is then sealed and placed in the facility's safe. It is kept there until you are released, or transferred.

Then you will be taken to have your fingerprints done and 'mug shots' taken, before being escorted to either a processing room to be issued jail clothes – or, if the staff are busy, you may be placed in the 'tank'. This is a large or small cell, with a number of other guys, all waiting to be processed. When you reach the processing area, that is where the dehumanising process starts. You begin to realise that you are no longer in control of your own life, not even of your own body. You are required to strip naked no matter how many other people are there. This is the standard procedure. Whether you were brought in for jaywalking or murder, it is all the same. It starts with the command to 'lift up your feet' in order to ensure you have nothing taped under them. Next, you are ordered to lift your arms up and run your hands through your hair, then run your fingers in and around your mouth. You are made to follow this sequence – lift your testicles, turn around and pull your arse cheeks apart, while squatting and coughing. There are times when you get a sadistic cop who will ask you to do the last two things, and then tell you to put your fingers in your mouth. Those who are real newbies will often fall for it, causing sniggering and laughs from those watching. The guys who have done time or who have a bit more sense will refuse, and they usually get left alone by the cops, who don't want a fight on their hands.

As most jails are overcrowded, when you first arrive in a cell block, you could find yourself having to sleep on the floor – in a cell, if you were lucky, or in the dayroom. This is often one of the most vulnerable times for those having their first taste of incarceration. Most people go into a general population cell block where there is a mixture of different types of crimes, usually drugs (using, possession, sales), robbery (petty, strong arm, armed), vandalism, car theft (joyriding, stripping for parts), drunk (in public, driving), forgery, assaults (simple, domestic violence), and even some sex crimes like statutory rape or date rape. Those who are in for the more serious sex crimes – forcible rape, sodomy, child molestation, for example, are placed in a protective housing area. Then you have those who are in for the most serious violent crimes – murder (1st degree, 2nd, conspiracy), attempted murder, assault with great bodily injury, arson, mayhem, who go to a secure housing area. It was in one of these Secure Housing

Units (SHUs), called 'High Power' that I found myself, because I met additional perceived security issues. Being an ex-military biker, I had a lot stacked against me.

I was placed in a four-man cell, but my arrival made me the sixth man. With only four bunks, it meant two of us would be sleeping on the floor. In the US, it is common to call Afro-Americans 'blacks' and Mexicans 'paisas'. Of the five already there, three were blacks and two were paisas. It turned out that I was known to one of the blacks, by way of his uncle who rode with a motorcycle club from south-side Fresno, and came to my shop. When he saw me, he threw the paisa off the upper bunk and told him he would be sleeping on the floor with the other paisa. Then he turned to one of the other blacks and asked him to move to the top, so I could have the bottom bunk. Such was the way of a SHU cell. Those who had the numbers decided on the sleeping arrangements. If the paisas had had the numbers, it would have played out differently. I was in a minority of one and in no position to argue.

It was at this time that I met a young white guy who had been given a tattoo by a couple of cousins. Unfortunately, this particular tattoo was getting him grief from many of the other inmates. He was just a skinny kid, and the tattoo on his left shoulder was a large rooster with a very visible erect penis. On one occasion, when we came out to take showers, I saw him being harassed. Me being me, I decided enough was enough. I waded into the group of four to five guys who were hassling him and told them to 'step up or step off'. After a couple of moments of grumbling, they all decided to walk away. I introduced myself to the kid and asked him about the tattoo. He explained he had wanted one, but his cousins got him drunk and instead of doing what he wanted, gave him this one as a joke. I decided to offer him some advice. I said, 'You know, instead of being ashamed of it, you ought to wear it as a badge of honour. When anyone asks you about it, tell them loud and proud – that's right, I am Rooster and I am the Cock O' the Walk. Then walk away and leave them with that thought.' He suddenly smiled, and I saw his shoulders go back. He now owned it and I knew he would be all right. Incredibly, 35 years later, he would contact me, after reading my first book – *34 Years in Hell* – and thank me for helping him.

Generally, in jails if you didn't have to go to any court proceedings, you would see most guys either sleeping or playing cards. In High Power, there was little room to work out, and the only time you got to go to the recreation yard on the top of the building was when it was either raining or above 100 degrees. There always seemed to be guards who were still experiencing the trauma of having their milk money taken in primary school, so now with power, they were getting revenge.

As the Fresno County Jail was not segregated by race, as I later discovered many in California were, it came as a shock to me when I found that the state prison system was. But here, we ate, slept, showered, and played cards together. That's not to say that there were no cell fights. In fact, some would end up with the person believed to be the aggressor going into administration segregation – solitary confinement, usually, for anywhere between a couple of days to a few months. Of course, if you went to Ad Seg, it would often bugger up your court case as the prosecutor could ask for more time so they could investigate whether they could press additional charges.

In fact, often while in the county jail awaiting trial, the prosecutor would add a slew of additional petty charges to pad the bill, so he could either make a jury believe you were worse than you really are, or to add leverage to force you to plea bargain out. The plea bargain is common in the US. Some crimes are punishable by such draconian sentences that people plea bargain and accept a lesser sentence for fear of what they might be sentenced to if they went to trial. That is what happened in my own case while I was in the county jail. I was told to plead guilty or else my wife would be facing a death sentence and execution. I ask you, what else could I do?

Chapter 2

A WORLD APART

The big day in jail, besides the one when you were sentenced, was the day you actually got sent to prison. When this came for me in February 1984, there were only two reception centres in California. If you were above Bakersfield, you went to the California Medical Facility (CMF) at Vacaville, and if you were below Bakersfield you went to California Institution for Men (CIM) at Chino. All women, no matter which part of the state they were from, went to the California Institution for Women (CIW). The bus ride from Fresno County Jail to the California Medical Facility only takes a couple of hours, but the experience of arriving through those gates at the prison is a whole world apart. The rules, politics and society you entered would be completely different to the one you had just left.

Despite the fact that you had already been in custody for months, once again you had to go through all the indignities you had at the jail, except here they are broadened. You had to stand for hours naked among other people while guards and inmate workers went about their jobs fully-clothed around you. Yes, you had to go through the whole lot – show your mouth, lift your balls and pull your arse cheeks apart for inspection at least three to four times during intake time. Then you are given clothes that may or may not be clean. Often the boxer shorts will have someone else's pubic hair in them, and the one sheet and two blankets all smell and are stained with an unknown source. Your guess is as good as mine. Next, they hand you what is called a 'fish kit' – because new inmates are termed 'fresh fish'. The fish kit consists of a bar of soap, tooth powder, a small, cheap toothbrush, comb, a toilet roll and a cheap razor. You are instructed that when you want new items, you have to turn in what remains of the old ones, even the cardboard inside the toilet roll. Welcome to your new existence!

And for the first-time prisoner, you quickly learn to be alert to everything going on around you. Even some of the most hardened, life-long criminals have a bit of apprehension or a sense of fear about going back inside. That may seem strange, but whether they have done one previous prison term or several, they knew each time they would be pulled back into the politics of those who they chose to run with. And that is because, outside their cell, on the yard, in the chow hall or in the gym, the prison gangs rule the roost.

But before reality sinks in, you get taken to a cell. Your cell is where you will live for however long it takes before somebody decides to transfer you out. The problem is, it isn't just your cell. It's an eight feet by four feet box you have to share with somebody else, somebody who is, 99 per cent of the time, a total stranger, and quite often somebody you would not give the time of day to on the outside. And sometimes that person will try to control the cell. You might arrive to find that they have a list of 'cell rules' that they expect you to obey. Fortunately, if everything in the prison is running well, and you have a work assignment, you could expect to only be in the cell for 10 hours a day, between the end of night yard and the morning unlock. But during lockdowns, you are stuck in your cell, with your 'celly', 24 hours a day. Lockdowns occur frequently, as trouble elsewhere in the prison, and sometimes even trouble in a different prison, will trigger them. Even the 9/11 event, despite the fact it happened on the East Coast, resulted in a lockdown that went on for weeks. The longest lockdown I endured was 18 months.

Your cell is very sparsely furnished. It has two bunks, one above the other, a metal sink and a metal toilet against the back wall at the end of the bottom bunk to give some semblance of privacy. But it doesn't have a cover to mask the smell. You are told that all you are permitted is six cubic feet of property. If the guards are being difficult, they can bring in a six feet by one foot by one foot box, commonly called the coffin, and woe betide you if everything you possess doesn't fit inside it.

Back in 1984, most prisons were designed with cells to hold two people. The size of the cell ranged from four feet by eight feet, to six feet by ten feet. They had a sink and toilet. The only exception, as I found out many years later, was that at DVI in the unit called L3, the cell had no sink or toilet and we had to use a communal area. Of course, as we had no facilities in the cell, it was not feasible to keep inmates locked in. Inmates could come and go to the toilet facilities without bothering the guards. It was only during count times and lockdown that guards would use a locking bar to prevent the cell doors from opening. To my knowledge, the only other place that allowed inmates to have keys to their cells was at CMC (California Men's Colony), but I have no idea why. In California, there were also the notorious dormitory blocks, where on average 200-300 men slept in a large warehouse-type environment, often in bunks three tiers high, a horrific experience that I endured for more than four years of my incarceration.

With no table/desk or chair, you have to sit on your bunk when you read, write or just ponder your situation. But your cell is pretty bare and to make it liveable, one way or another, you have to acquire some home comforts. They all come at a cost, some are permitted, and others are frowned on by the guards. They also come with a cell search, as they can be deemed contraband and confiscated.

So, gradually, you have to accumulate a few possessions to make your life more bearable. The big problem is they all cost money. If you are not lucky enough to have family or friends on the outside who will pay into your prison account, the only way you can get funds is by getting a job, and nothing pays as much as $1 an hour, or you can work out a hustle to make yourself some money.

Probably highest on your list of wants is a TV or radio to help pass the time. These can be bought legally, for a price, from either an approved supplier via a catalogue, or even, the prison canteen. The TV or radio becomes your property and has your prison number engraved on it. But they are expensive, something like $100 for a radio and $200 for a TV. Prisoners only earn about 20 cents an hour, so can't afford that kind of expense. This opens up the underground market that is rampant in prisons. They buy or rent from another prisoner, who might be upgrading or has acquired a set from somebody who has paroled out and doesn't want theirs. Of course, it comes with the other prisoner's number on, which leaves you open to all kinds of problems should the guards decide to do a thorough cell search and check on the number on your TV.

But TVs and radios are not the only things you can get from other inmates instead of from the prison-approved way. These include stingers, little immersion heaters used to heat a cup of water for your coffee or your packet of ramen soup. The ones you can obtain legally for $10 are low voltage and take at least five minutes to heat up your water, but illegally from other prisoners you can get one built to heat a five-gallon bucket to a boil in two to three minutes and only costs $5.

A five-gallon bucket was a desired item, usually smuggled out from the kitchens. It could be used for washing clothes, but was also useful if you were in the business of making the prison drink, 'pruno'. The bucket could also be turned upside down, with a folded blanket on top to make a seat. A blessed change from having to sit on your bunk all the time, and a relief to whoever had the top bunk in your cell! If you were sitting on your lower bunk, you might suddenly find your celly's feet in your face if they chose to sit up and put their legs over the side of their bunk.

Extra bedding was also very desired. Even Californian nights can be very, very cold. The official allowance was one very thin mattress, one sheet, two blankets, a pillowcase, but no pillow. Nobody ever explained that one! It took ingenuity to find the materials to make up a pillow, but the longer I was inside, the more resourceful I became.

To brighten your life, you could buy in from other prisoners, or make for yourself, picture frames or keepsake boxes from either cigarette pack wrappers or lolly sticks. One of my favourite hustles was to use lolly sticks to make model motorcycles or small Dungeons and Dragons figures, which was very profitable as it was a popular game within the prison world. Of course, it is illegal for actual cash to be held by any prisoner, so payment between prisoners comes in the form of canteen or cosmetic items, or you might be offered tobacco or drugs.

Many of the things you can get in this underground market came with a very big risk. Anything that was not purchased through the approved manner could be deemed 'contraband' and confiscated. It could also carry a real risk of further punishment and even a spell in Ad Seg. It all depended on the guards and whether they turned a blind eye or decided to enforce the rules.

But how does an inmate get around a Californian

prison? By a system of ducats and passes. No, not gold coins! The ducat was a one-off pass needed to go to most places away from your housing unit, except the yard, chow hall and your work assignment. Ducats were either issued by your housing guard, or whichever member of staff who wanted to see the inmate. The most likely ones you would receive would be to see your counsellor, go to medical, library, package room, psychologists, self-help groups and the dreaded parole board hearings. To get to your daily regular ports of call, you would have a separate pass, which was specific only for the place of destination, for example, where you worked.

Chapter 3

CHOW TIME

You learn pretty quickly where your chow hall is, otherwise, unless you came in with money, you would starve to death. These were run differently at each prison. Usually, they would seat between 100-200 people at a time. At some prisons, with large populations, they would have several chow halls running with 15 minutes to eat, so the next group could get in. Some prisons would allow you to sit where you liked, others would make you take the next available seat, regardless of which other races were already seated at the table of four. A few prisons had designated tables and rows for different races and often used the 'whites' and 'others' inmates as buffers between the groups that were at war.

When I first went to prison, in 1984, the chow halls gave us our food on metal trays and we had a metal spoon and fork, all of which you had to return after your meal under the watchful eye of a guard stationed at the exit door. It was not surprising that occasionally one of the utensils would get smuggled out and turned into a weapon. If a fight broke out in the chow hall itself, any fork could instantly turn into a lethal instrument, and stabbings were not uncommon. Worse, some inmates had learned that if you dropped the metal tray to the floor, you could use the concrete to flatten an edge and sharpen it into a blade. The tray could then be thrown like a discus, and the edge was sharp enough to peel through somebody's scalp. It took until the 1990s before the authorities changed everything to plastic.

All prisons, even though they are given the same approved menus and the same ingredients from their Sacramento headquarters, do not turn out the same quality food as even the big burger restaurant chains. You have some food managers who believe it is their sacred duty to feed the inmates on the lowest budget possible. Others actually try to get the biggest bang for their buck, and it is those I give my props to. It has been said that if prison officials want to have the smoothest running prisons, there are four things that will help accomplish that – hot water, regular visiting, timely mail delivery and decent food. I will agree on all of those, though in my experience it would be decent food that would be the biggest help.

Many prison meals were less concerned with being

nutritious and more with trying to provide the right number of calories for a day's intake.

So here are a few examples of our meals, taken straight from menus I sent home for my pen pal.

Breakfast	*Lunch*	*Dinner*
Apple	Peanut butter	Chicken cheese supreme
Oatmeal	Jelly	Rice
Cream beef	Bread	Carrots
Biscuit	Cookies	Cornbread
Diced potatoes	Apple	Jello
Juice	Bagel dog	Goulash on noodles
Grits	Mustard	Pinto beans
Donut holes	Crisps	Cornbread
Peanut butter	Apple	Pudding

(With breakfast we got milk / coffee – lunch and dinner, it was Kool-Aid).

This shows that the prison kitchens were only concerned about filling us up and, as my pen pal would tell me, with some strange food combinations to British eyes.

Peanuts were a constant in our diet, as we would get peanut butter at least eight to ten times a week. I found it amazing that in 34½ years, I never heard of a single allergic reaction, which made me wonder, does somehow being allergic to peanuts keep a person from committing crimes? Those who claimed to be vegetarians would be given even more peanut butter or beans instead of meat. Up until the middle of the 1990s, we were still getting 'real' meat, and most prisons had their own butcher shops. But over the next 10-15 years, they would serve virtually no meat and instead went with a soy substitute which they could flavour however they wished, usually chicken, turkey or beef.

Another thing that was done regularly was to make peanut brittle. This was done by first scraping off all the paint from the bottom corner of a steel sheet bunk, then using an antacid bottle with some baby oil purchased from the canteen, and a cotton string from the mop, so you could make a cooker. Then you had to smuggle back from the chow hall butter, peanut butter and syrup from breakfast and add peanuts bought from the canteen. Then you get some books to help position the cooker to the right height under the bunk and you light the wick by either using matches given out with the smoking supplies or you had to 'pop a socket', which is done by wrapping toilet paper around the bend in a paper clip shaped into a 'U'.

When the tip is pushed into a socket the toilet paper bursts into flames and hey presto, you have a light! Of course, usually you got an electric shock as well, but that was something you learned to live with. Once you have the cooker heating up the scraped area, you put some butter on to test how hot it is, you want it to just start to sizzle. Having made a slightly pourable mixture of the peanut butter, peanuts and syrup, you spread it thinly over the heated area and allow it to start to cook, keeping the heat on it until the syrup begins to crystallise. Then put out the cooker (save for another day), and let the mixture cool down once it has set for about an hour. You take a shoe and from underneath the bunk you begin to bang it until the peanut brittle cracks & breaks into pieces. Then enjoy! The guys who were really good at making it often traded some for coffee, soups or soap bought in the canteen. As you can see, already, in the county jail, you are learning to adjust to life on the inside, learning how to deal with those around you, and working out little hustles to make some money on the side and your time more bearable. It's useful preparation for what lies ahead.

Chapter 4

DANGER IN THE SHOWERS

Another aspect of prison life that you quickly had to come to terms with, particularly in parts of California where the temperature can be more than 100 degrees for days on end, is the need to keep clean and/or cool down. There are no baths in the prison system, so your days of having a long, relaxing soak soon become a distant memory. The answer in prison is showers. Some prisons had showers in the yard, supposedly for inmates to use after working out. But you soon found that their use was only for those willing and able to guarantee their own protection. At Folsom, it was in the showers on the yard that many gang members were attacked by those of their own group who were supposed to be protecting them. Showers in the housing units were always a communal affair. Most of the time, they were called

'Gang Showers'. An old guard at Folsom in 1984 told me that as inmate work crews were made into gangs of 6-12, inmates would always shower together – and the shower areas always had 6-12 shower heads. In some newer prisons, there would be a post with four heads on and inmates were so close together that they could hook arms if they wished. Most often they would just bump arses and shoulders. However, if any soap or shampoo suds fell on another person, especially of another race, it could start a fight. Soap-on-a-rope became fashionable as having to bend over and pick up a bar of soap from the floor was not ideal.

The rule of thumb at most prisons was that if you went to the yard when your housing unit was having shower time inside, you had to shower in the yard instead. But if you were at a prison that didn't have yard showers and were out at shower time, then your only option was to take what was called a 'whore's bath' using the sink in your cell.

The one exception was if you had a job where there was a single shower unit that your boss unofficially allowed you to use. This was most often available only if you were a clerk in the administration office for an associate warden, captain, lieutenant or sergeant and, in some cases, vocational shops. They probably didn't want to smell sweaty bodies where they were working, but it was appreciated because it was a luxury as you could often control the temperature and pressure of the spray, and not have to rush.

One of the other biggest drawbacks to taking showers in prison was being under the gaze of other inmates, guards and even individuals who were just touring the prison. Though, most complaints came when female guards were watching and making certain comments.

Privacy is a privilege you don't have in prison. You also have to adapt to the fact that there are expectations among prisoners, one being that you never have a bowel movement after your cellmate has gone to sleep, and even during the daytime you are expected to keep flushing the toilet in order to keep the smell down. Many cell fights have happened over toilet use, or even passing wind. The small confined space demands that you have to respect each other.

The first stabbing I saw at Folsom was just a few days after I arrived, on the yard. Folsom did not have the largest yard, in fact the running track, which sat in almost the centre of the yard, was quite disappointing. The first time I became aware of the running track was from a movie, called *The Jericho Mile*, in which Peter Strauss played a lifer who would constantly run the track. He could run great distances with little effort, and faster than many Olympic athletes on the outside. There is a point in the movie where the warden authorises the building of a regulation one-mile track on Folsom's yard, so he might be given the opportunity to represent the United States. From having seen the film, I thought the place would be a lot grander than it was in reality.

On the yard, just north of the running track is #1 building and at the end of that building, to the west, there is an asphalt outdoor recreation area with tables, bolted to the ground to they can't be used as weapons, on which inmates can play cards and dominoes, or just sit and talk (and, yes, these tables were segregated on the grounds of race or gang). This area was given the name 'Blood Alley' due to the number of assaults and stabbings. Generally there would be at least one incident a day. The most dangerous spot on the yard was at the very north end of Blood Alley, where the inmate yard showers were. Prison rules stated that if you went to the yard, you would have to take a shower there rather than inside the building that you lived in. I saw more than a dozen men brought out from the shower area after they had been stabbed during the nine months I was at Folsom State Prison for the first time.

When members of different gangs went to take showers, they would have one or two fellow gang members posting up to make sure that no rival gang could do them harm. Sadly, in more than a few cases, it would be those who had been sent to protect the guy who would actually have been given the green light by their shot caller to stab the person for some transgression. I happened to be at the very front of Blood Alley when I saw an inmate come staggering from the direction of the Greystone Chapel. He had a large red blossom starting to show on his white T-shirt. Immediately loudspeakers started yelling the order, 'get down, get down, all convicts get down.' This was followed by a warning shot fired into the air by the guards on the gun walk above Blood Alley. Though I did immediately get down, I could see the bleeding inmate struggling to breathe and my first instinct, having been a Navy Corpsman, was to run to him and try to save his life.

However, the moment I started to rise from the ground, this old lifer knocked my foot out from under me and laid on top of me while telling me, 'we don't run towards bleeding people.' I said I had been a corpsman and that I thought I could help him. The old lifer looked at me and said, 'If you go to help him, who's going to help you when you get shot by the guards, They will be thinking that you are on your way to stab him up some more.' This was my indoctrination into life at Folsom. There would have to be at least three stabbings on the yard for staff to recall the yard and return us to our cells.

Chapter 5

GANGS ON THE YARD

Your next experience out of your cell is probably the prison yards. They tend to be basically the same at every institution. There is always a main yard for the general population, and one for the Ad Seg inmates. At a prison where inmates of different custody levels would be kept separate, there would be a yard for each group. As for Ad Seg units, I observed the evolution of these from an open yard to being a sectioned-off fenced dog run, where separate racial and gang groups could be placed side by side without harming each other. Many prisons place small cages of about six feet wide by eight feet long so each holds only one person. Even within a group, members might attack each other for a number of reasons. Most yards had weight piles, the politics of which I will discuss further in a later chapter when I talk about the gangs in prison, and some are big enough for a running track around their perimeter.

Apart from recreation, another reason to go to the main yard was to go to the canteen, chapel, package room or counsellor's office, which could be accessed that way, without the need for an internal pass. The yard may give you fresh air, but it is not the place to let down your guard, unless you are with trusted friends and even then, you need to keep your eyes open because, in prison, can you really trust anyone at all?

In California, even if you have never put a foot wrong, you are aware that gangs exist. Prison gangs and street gangs, they both wield a lot of power, and a lot of people are frightened of them. So, for most guys going into prison, they feel the need to join up with one or the other of these gangs – usually depending on their race, the area they are from or even their religion in the case of Muslims. It is often said that they join a gang to gain protection from the other gangs. There are relatively few, like myself, who make a conscious decision not to join a gang, as they just want to do their time and get out when they are supposed to – something that may not happen if you 'click up'. But the gangs don't make it easy for you, because all the time each gang feels the need to be shown 'honour' and 'respect,' and if you are not one of them, then you must be one of their enemies.

There is a real misunderstanding in prison, and perhaps out in the free world as well, when it comes to how the words 'honour' and 'respect' are interpreted inside prison. You hear them thrown about an awful lot on the inside, generally by the gangs. After I came home, I was surprised to find so many people on the internet praising the prison gangs. This told me that either they knew nothing about the way the gangs operate, or based their opinions only on what they had seen in movies. There is the possibility they may have been to prison themselves and actually became gang members. But as gangs run like a pyramid with the elite few at the top and the weak poor fodder at the bottom, it would suggest they had been forced to fall in line out of fear or, worse yet, the 'need to belong'. Either way, they still have no idea what the words 'honour' and 'respect' actually mean.

Each gang demands 'respect', most often because of their race or where they are from. Of course, they won't give the same to other prisoners not of their group. However, even within their group, those at the bottom of the pecking order are given little respect, and are expected to do all the menial tasks such as carrying drugs and contraband such as knives, syringes, and pipes. If found on a prisoner, all will result in time in Ad Seg and probably an enhancement of their sentence. These lower orders find themselves being forced to clean the senior members' cells, steal things the group needs, being sent to do 'hits' (stabbings or beatings on prisoners who may have offended the elite in some way), and even to get into physical altercations with guards to allow senior members time to get away from a bad situation. And yes, they can even be expected to provide sexual relief to a more senior member.

'Honour' is another word which has lost meaning to gangs. Once I had a shot caller – the gang member senior enough to order the others around – tell me that when they have to roll up on someone (attack a person), they have to make sure they have the numbers present so they can win, as there was no honour in losing. This conversation came about when I questioned why it took 10 of them to attack an 80-year-old guy who had, in his thirties and forties, been a hitter for their gang. They were so unsure of themselves, they had to overpower this old guy for the sake of their honour. This is what happened with Whitey Bulger, an old gangster confined to a wheelchair. He was attacked by three guys carrying knives, who succeeded in killing him. Is this really the mark of honour? Back in the 1950s to early 80s, someone who had served the gang properly was able to 'retire' without any stigma, but that changed drastically in the 90s, when an old guy was just seen as weak and a victim to be taken advantage of. As I pointed out when Whitey Bulger was killed, it is easier for three to four guys to take out someone in a wheelchair than stand toe-to-toe with someone in their prime and who has the heart to say, 'I don't want to join your prison gang'.

The 'white' gangs in California have a real warped sense of what is right and wrong for a white guy to do. For example, a 'white' is not supposed to take food from another race if offered, yet it is often other races who put the food on your chow hall tray. You are not allowed to drink from the same cup or work out on the same weight pile in the yard as another race, yet it is all right for the shot callers to buy and use the drugs that came out of another race's arse. How does that make any sense? The white gangs have no problem pressuring whites who are only doing a short bit of time or those who just show weakness to have their family members smuggle drugs into the prison. The families are usually told that their loved one will be killed if they don't do as ordered, or if they tell the authorities. So, mothers, wives, girlfriends and even grandmothers have been pulled into this situation. Sadly, there were even times when the drugs were hidden in an infant's diaper in the hope it wouldn't be discovered in a search. Eventually these 'mules' are caught and do prison time as well. If children are involved, they are taken into care and lost to the system, with the chance they may very well become the next generation of inmates.

There was a thing called the 'Convict Code', which only seemed to be used by the whites. It was even common to see it tattooed on their chests or backs. Convict Code – 'If I Lead Follow Me, If I Hesitate Push Me, If I Tell Kill Me'. I don't know where it originated from, though by the mid-2000s when the prison system had opened their 'Special Programming Units' (SPU), there were a number of white gang dropouts with that saying tattooed on them who had become disillusioned by gang life and didn't want anyone to carry out the last bit of the Code – 'If I Tell Kill Me'. To drop out of a gang, they had to tell, as was required to get into SPU, which had replaced the Sensitive Needs Yards (SNY) of the late 1980s-2000, which was supposed to provide for those with a need for secure housing, though many people still died while supposedly being protected from the gangs.

'Are you white?' That is the most important question posed to those confronted by white supremacists when they arrive on a prison yard. I always found it strange, as no other group walks up and asks, 'Are you black, are you Hispanic or are you Asian?' They might ask where someone comes from, their state, county, city or neighbourhood, but never what colour they are. You might think that telling if someone is 'white', might be relatively easy, but you would be wrong. When I asked the question, 'How do you know someone is white?' to a skinhead named Dreamer, his response was 'Because they say they are'. It really depended on a number of things. I saw people of Middle Eastern heritage with dark swarthy skin, black eyes and dark tightly-curled hair, running as white and when I was at Deuel Vocational Institution (DVI), the skinheads had a shot caller called Bubba Hernandez, who claimed he was 100 per cent white and that only his father was Mexican. Even at Folsom State Prison, the Aryan Brotherhood had within its number a couple of Jewish guys who found it far easier to become 'white' than be Jewish. This meant that they got the proper tattoos, such as lightning bolts, swastikas on their necks and hands, with Heil Hitler or even Nazi warbirds emblazed on their chest or back. It seemed that the colour of skin, hair, eyes and accents had little bearing on whether someone was truly white. If you didn't answer the question quickly enough or in a sensible manner, there was the chance of a fight, as the person asking might think you were trying to hide something.

I was also amazed at how many whites had wives or girlfriends who were either part, or in some cases full-blooded, Asians, Hispanics or Native American. I always wondered if they so badly needed to hate someone, that they would choose to have a relationship and possibly have children who could never be 'pure,' or was this just another act of more hypocrisy.

The concern that people might be trying to hide why they were in prison brought about, in the early 1990s, the request or demand to 'See your paperwork' from gang leaders. It meant you had to pull out your charge sheets from court and show it to whoever asked. If you didn't have it, you could get smashed right there by those asking and, almost always, it would be a group attacking you. If you could sound convincing enough, they might give you a couple of days to see your prison counsellor and get a copy. Of course, depending on your charges, you could still find yourself being beaten down to the point of having to go to the hospital or even having to request protective housing.

In the hierarchy of the prison system murderers were seen at the top and child molesters (Cho Mos) were at the bottom. However, it wasn't quite so cut and dried as killing with a gun, knife or fist were really high up, unless the victim was elderly, a woman or a child. Then you were placed in a lower category to even a person with just an assault. Even among those who were in for arson, there was a separate ranking, with those who did it for insurance reasons (even if hired by business owners) at the top and those who did it for thrills at the bottom. Those who hurt children were always at the bottom and constantly had to worry they would be attacked, not just by other inmates, but staff as well.

There were a lot of reasons for why someone might need protective housing. The most common reasons after being a child molester were (in no particular order), drug or gambling debts to other prisoners, telling the guards about illegal activities you knew were going down, both inside and outside of prison, and wanting to drop out of your gang.

The fastest way to lock up off a prison yard was to get stabbed. However, if the reason was drugs and gambling debts, the prison staff would just move you to another prison. For some reason, the guards thought the debts would not follow you, which they often would, or the person would get into more debt at the new prison. The person would have to find themselves getting stabbed at two or three prisons before staff would take it seriously enough to give them protective housing. I knew of one guy who had been stabbed 58 times from assaults at different prisons – the guards used to call him 'pincushion' – before he found his way into protective custody.

When I first went to prison in 1984, you didn't get asked to show your paperwork because you didn't need to! At that time, the California prison system used something called a 103B card. This went from prison to prison with you and was kept in R&R (Receiving and Releasing Unit). It told your name, date of birth, race, county of commitment, charges and how long you were sentenced. Up until 1990, most prisons had inmates working in R&R as clerks and porters who had full access to the 103B cards.

This allowed the word on new arrivals to be out to the yard before they were even assigned cells.

At some point in my prison time, I did come across and had to deal with members of just about every one of these groups and as with any organisation, there were reasonable guys and ones you needed to keep an eye on. I only dealt with most as the job I was doing at the time dictated (clerk, surgical tech, hobby shop, etc) and did not compromise my integrity or sense of honour, I found I had little to worry about – not that I was safe, far from it. It was often the person who felt safe who would most likely become a victim. I was always on guard and ready to 'hold my mud,' as I had learned from the US Military. In the toilet area on the yard, gang members had others watching out for them at every vulnerable moment. That is how hazardous life can be in prison.

It is important to know and understand that gangs, in whatever form they take, do not have or teach socially redeeming skills to their members, so it benefits them more to have their people inside rather than out of prison. I am going to list some of the major prison and street gangs that a new inmate might find themselves confronted by, and hopefully this will give you a better understanding as to why the world behind the granite wall or double rows of electrified fences was at all times a dangerous and unforgiving place.

Chapter 6

WHO'S WHO IN GANGLAND

Gangs can take over your life from the moment you arrive in prison, but of the individual gangs in California prisons, not all of them started in prison. There are a lot of factions in the street gangs who will fight against each other on the streets of where they live, yet join together once in prison, forming a temporary truce. Some street gangs will also 'ride' with a prison gang while inside, only to completely separate from them once they go back outside.

They basically break down as follows:

Mexican Mafia or 'Eme' – which is the Spanish pronunciation for the letter M. As 'M' is the 13th letter of the alphabet, they will often get a tattoo of the number 13 or 'XIII' usually somewhere very visible using the colour blue to identify themselves, often wearing blue bandanas, hats or shoes. They were the first gang recognised by the prison authorities when they formed in the 1950s at Deuel Vocational Institution and are mostly composed of Hispanics from the southern part of the state, either US born or raised, though they do have some caucasian members. The first white to join them was Joe Morgan, more commonly known as 'Peg Leg Joe', due to his prosthetic leg. Born of Croatian parents, raised in a Hispanic area, he joined the Ford Maravilla street gang and became fluent in Spanish. He eventually rose to a senior rank with the Eme, and it was his negotiating skills that formed a loose alliance with the Aryan Brotherhood in defence against the Nuestra Familia and their black gang associates.

Nuestra Familia (Our Family) – as N is the 14th letter of the alphabet, this gang tattooed the number 14 on themselves, though usually adapting the Roman numerals 'XIV', using the colour red to identify themselves. They originally formed in the northern part of the state and first became established at California Training Facility (CTF) – Soledad in the 1960s. You will hear them called 'Nortenos' by the prison staff and other non-Hispanic inmates. They will ally with black gangs when there is a power struggle at a prison, though surprisingly there are some northern prisons where they cannot go because those are controlled by the Mexican Mafia (Surenos), one of which was Folsom State Prison.

The Black Guerrilla Family was founded in 1966 at San Quentin Prison by George L. Jackson, a former Black Panther. It is the only black prison gang recognised by the California authorities, and its purpose was originally political. What set the BGF apart from others was that they were very proactive in having their members educate themselves, as they were more politically minded than other gangs. For quite a while, they required their members to read the book by Sun Tzu, *The Art of War*. This book has not only been used by the military, but also by businesses.

The Aryan Brotherhood originated in San Quentin Prison in 1964. This gang was formed by members of an earlier gang called 'The Bluebirds', who had started as a way for whites to protect themselves from other races. Once they evolved into the AB, they took on a new mission, which was to try to control drugs coming into the prisons. As they used extremely violent methods in their attempt to become a power behind the walls, ultimately all white gangs in prison pay a certain homage to the AB. It is prison policy that all 'validated'

AB shot callers and full members are placed in indeterminate SHU (Security Housing Unit) programmes in maximum security prisons such as Pelican Bay, and yet they still are calling shots from there and prison officials cannot seem to control the flow of information.

Fresno Bulldogs – Initially they were just called 'F14ers' when I grew up in Fresno and were a part of the Nortenos. Starting in the mid-1960s, many did wear bulldog tattoos, which were the mascot symbols for both Fresno State University and Fresno City College, though they were not an independent group until the 1980s. Breaking ranks with the Nortenos happened in 1986, when they decided they were tired of being used as pawns by the Nortenos and chose to go to war with them. This was referred to by prison authorities as the 'The Red Wave', as it washed over all the prisons where Bulldogs and Nortenos were housed. They now all use a bulldog paw print and bulldog head image in their tattoos and artwork. It is common for gang members to call each other 'Dog' or 'Perro' (Spanish for dog). They have no allies in or out of prison, choosing to run independently and claiming neither Surenos nor Nortenos affiliation. In 2006, there was an unsuccessful attempt by law enforcement agencies to wipe out the Bulldogs, as they were controlling the majority of the distribution of methamphetamine, marijuana, and heroin not only in Fresno County, but into other areas in the Central valley. Even with the more than 2,400 arrests of Bulldogs and associates, it had little effect in curtailing their activities.

San Jose Sharks – A semi-autonomous faction within the Nortenos, who tend to engage against the Fresno Bulldogs. One way they insult them is to tattoo a shark (usually a great white) with a bulldog in its mouth.

The Nazi Lowriders – (NLR or The Ride) are a white prison gang who has established itself as a criminal organisation in Southern California and Texas. They tend to be allies with the Aryan Brotherhood and Mexican Mafia. Their main rivals are the Bloods, Crips, BGF and the Nuestra Familia. Their drug of choice is methamphetamine which has often fuelled their violence, not only with the public but police officers too. They have gained notoriety through the prison staff and are seen as potentially more dangerous than the AB were in their heyday. Once an inmate is identified as an active member of the NLR, he is removed from the general prison population and placed in an indeterminate SHU status. What makes them unique, as a white gang, is that they have developed contacts with other white organisations throughout the West Coast, including the Ku Klux Klan.

Peckerwoods – This is not a single gang, but a grouping of the many independent white groups who tattoo the word 'Peckerwood' on themselves. The term is a racial slur which originated in the 1830s, prominently used in the southern United States to identify especially rural poor whites. One definition has been given as 'weak, poor white trash'. It is actually on par with using the 'N' word for identifying those of African descent. What I could never understand is that both groups called members in their group by these derogatory names. Many white prisoners proudly call themselves 'Peckerwood' and it is one of the more common tattoos found on white inmates throughout the United States. Women who run with this group are called 'Featherwoods'. Those wearing the Peckerwood tattoo may often belong to other white supremacist groups or gangs as well. Some of the better-known factions of white gangs that fall under this title go by the name of Nor Cal Peckerwoods, Sacramaniacs (from Sacramento County), and the Fresnecks (from Fresno County). All the Peckerwood gangs seem to come under the direction of the Nazi Lowriders who, in turn, often receive orders directly from the AB who are operating from Pelican Bay SHU.

The Green Wall – Strangely, this gang is solely made up of prison guards! It is believed to have started around Thanksgiving Day 1996 at Salinas Valley State Prison, near Soledad, California. Though most guards never officially joined, they would often turn a blind eye to the activities of those who were members. Some of the activities attributed to members of the Green Wall were to stage fights between rival gang members (videoing to show to others and even sell), placing vulnerable (though uncooperative) inmates in cells with those they knew would brutalise, both physically and sexually, the weaker inmates.

Street Gangs – You may not think that the street gangs could have the same influence inside as the prison gangs, but they do. If they want a prisoner to do something, they can bring pressure to bear on family members outside the walls. In 2019, the US Department of Justice recognised at least 450 street gangs, with the majority originating in Los Angeles, now nick-named the 'gang capital of America'. The State of California Department of Corrections and Rehabilitation has acknowledged that Deuel Vocational Institution has produced the most state prison gangs. It can be confidently stated that most street gangs across the US can trace their roots back to California. When members of these gangs came to prison, they were often recruited by the established prison gangs to be used as foot soldiers. However, even though they realised they were being exploited, they knew it would increase their status and standing when they got out, as they had earned some stripes while inside.

Crips – So named because they like to cripple people. This is an African-American gang based in the coastal regions throughout Southern California, though they were originally founded in Los Angeles in 1969. By 2000, there were more than 600 Crips factions in operation. They are considered to be one of the largest and most violent of the street gangs, as they have opened up branches in virtually every major city across the whole of the US and Canada. It is said they have in excess of 35,000 members and have been involved in murders, robberies, prostitution, and drug dealing. There is a bitter rivalry between Crips and the Bloods. Their most famous member, and one of the founders, is Stanley 'Tookie' Williams. In 1979, as a member of the West Side Crips, he was involved in a gang war with other factions of Crips. Williams was arrested for four murders and eventually sent to Death Row in San Quentin. They use blue as the colour to identify themselves to others.

Bloods (Pirus) – Initially, in 1969, the Pirus were created by young Blacks out of Compton CA who had been victimised by the Crips. They created their own gang, called the Piru Street Family or the Piru Gangsters. In 1974, LA County Jail members of the Pirus and the Brims formed an alliance and created the Bloods. They all wear the colours of red or burgundy regardless if they are Bloods or Pirus and continue to this day to fight with the Crips over drugs and territory.

18th Street Gang – This is a multi-ethnic group composed largely of Central Americans and Mexicans. They have been known to recruit outside the Hispanic community. When they started to battle with more established Hispanic gangs, there were more than 200 separate individual gangs working under the same name within separate areas of the San Fernando Valley, San Gabriel Valley, Riverside, Long Beach and many areas throughout Los Angeles. In the beginning, they were made up of mostly second-generation Hispanic immigrants. This gang was among one of the first to expand their membership to include other nationalities and races in Los Angeles. The US Justice Department has listed them as one of the largest trans-national criminal gangs in Los Angeles, with around 30-50,000 members in 20 states across the US alone. They are often allied with the Mexican Mafia (Eme). These two gangs alone have turned the Central American Northern Triangle into a region with the highest murder rate in the world. In the last 10 years, the 18th Street Gang have become even more dangerous as they groom young members within the US military, actively recruiting those already serving. This activity has allowed them to procure military armaments and skills they would not otherwise have been able to access. The 18th Street Gang has been identified to operate in Spain, Australia, Canada, England, France, Germany, Lebanon, Peru, the Philippines as well as many countries in Central America. It is occasionally referred to as 'The Children's Army' because of its known recruitment of schoolchildren. While their main source of income is the street level distribution of drugs, many members have been arrested and convicted of murder, assaults, arson, copyright infringement, extortion/human trafficking, illegal immigration (both into the US and Europe), kidnapping/prostitution and weapon trafficking.

Chapter 7

FEAR IN THE AIR

In prison, nearly anything you can think of can be used as a weapon. At some prisons, the thought and concern for one's own safety is constant. The feeling of fear is hanging in the air. You can see in the eyes of the other inmates the same wariness you might find in a deer or other prey animal. Particularly when I was at Folsom, San Quentin and Deuel Vocational Institution, there was a constant awareness of the need to be safe. The wearing of homemade armour under your jacket was quite common, so common in fact, that the library wasn't able to keep phone books on the shelves, as they were prized material to turn into stab-resistant vests. Thick magazines, such as *National Geographic* made great protection for your arms. When it comes to your life, you couldn't be too cautious. Not that everyone needed such defences, but if word went down that there was trouble brewing on the yard, or that somebody was looking for you, then it was best to be protected as best you could.

Learning how to fashion some form of self-protection and how to make weapons is something you learn pretty early on if you want to survive. It may be that as there are so many veterans within the prison system, some methods of weapon construction originally came in with them from their survival training. Or, as they say, 'Necessity is the mother of invention', and men who have plenty of time on their hands can learn to be inventive.

I have seen the simplest weapons made from just a straightened piece of fence wire that had been sharpened, or even a blade from a disposable razor that had been melted onto the end of a toothbrush handle. The latter was once used to slice me across the back of my right hand in a fight at Pleasant Valley State Prison. Unfortunately for the guy using it, the blade came off the handle after the first cut, and he found himself on the defensive side of the fight.

You may have heard the term in some prison movies or TV shows, 'lock in a sock'. Many prisons didn't allow inmates to have locks or the lock was so small it wouldn't do much damage. More often, someone would put multiple bars of soap in a sock. Believe me, if you get hit with a sock carrying eight to 10 bars of soap, especially on the head, you are not only left stunned but you also end up with soap dust in your eyes. When the prison canteen used to sell canned goods, guys would buy 1lb cans of chilli and drop two in a sock. They certainly did some damage when hitting someone.

When I first went into prison, we were able to buy all sorts of things in metal cans and often the lids, when cut off with a P-38 can opener, would have a sharp edge ideal for slashing. Guys would bend the lid in half and place it in an orange or grapefruit peel, then sneak up on someone and reach around them and begin to slice with a backstroke. They would try to blind the person or at least severely disfigure them. This was most often the weapon of choice used against those who faced charges which were not popular on most yards. At Avenal, some whites protected a paedophile because he could fix their radios. He tried to make a move on me using this very method. The moment I saw an arm come across my face and feel a body up against me, I brought up my right arm and prevented any serious damage. Although he was able to make a small cut across the tip of my nose and another on my cheek, I was able to disarm him and pin him to the floor. He told me who had sent him and then he chose to lock up − opt for administrative segregation − as did most of those involved. So, luckily for me, I only ended up with a couple of small scars.

Time moved on, and the powers that be finally worked out that they shouldn't be selling anything that could be turned into weapons. Canned goods now come in plastic packaging.

It was common for someone to get their wig split on the weight pile, even by their own race or gang. The aggressor would pick up a dumbbell, 30-50lb seemed to be the favourite, and sneak up while the victim was working out on a bench. With just a crack on the head, not only did the victim get injured from the blow, but whatever weights they were lifting would fall back down on them as well. Sometimes, the purpose was not to kill the victim, but to show that someone was upset with them. In that case, it would be a dumbbell slammed onto their testicles while benching, or even slamming it against one of their hands. I have actually seen a number of guys who, during a riot, had been hit in the head by a flying 5-10lb weight plate. Although they survived, they were left with a permanent dent in their heads where the plate had struck, and were never quite as functional as before.

One of the simplest, though deadly, weapons was made from Styrofoam cups and cling film. Cling film would be laid out on a flat surface and the cup would be set alight, allowing for it to melt and drip onto the cling film. Once there was a good amount spread across the cling film and while the Styrofoam was still malleable, it was rolled up to give it a point. The process would be repeated, except before you started rolling again, the previously rolled one would be placed in the centre and rolled around it. This would be done over and over until the right thickness was achieved. When it had hardened, it could be sharpened to a point, which would then be attached to a rolled up newspaper shaft creating a spear, which could be used to stab an inmate or guard through the cell bars with a good degree of efficiency. These had been very successful and could not be detected by a metal detector, which allowed them to be easily transported around the prison.

Those who were very serious about wanting to kill someone would usually make a knife, which could be made from broken glass, Plexiglas (most often shaped on a grinder or with sandpaper), or even cut out of the sheet metal plate that made up our bunks. The second day I was at Folsom in 1984, I happened to walk by a cell and saw an inmate feverishly working away, cutting out a blade from his bunk. As we did not have easy access to hacksaw blades, the way to do that was to take waxed dental floss and saturate the wax with an abrasive cleaning powder (often that was the tooth powder they gave to inmates who couldn't afford toothpaste). Once you wore a small hole in the metal bunk by either using a nail, screw or a pair of tweezers, you just fed the dental floss through the hole and started slowly sawing out the pattern you had drawn. It was not very easy and took quite a while, while hoping the cell would not get searched before it was finished.

You might be wondering if the guards ever noticed the missing piece of bunk. If a guard did spot it, they would log it and then an investigation would be carried out. The inmate or inmates who lived in the cell would get a disciplinary write-up and go to Ad Seg. The guard would paint the area around the missing bunk piece red. A guy I saw making a knife used some red paint he had procured, so to any guard it would look like it had been previously discovered and investigated.

Knives were not the only weapons used as there were a lot of very inventive guys on the inside. Things like match bombs and methane bombs (they would fart into thin latex gloves they would get from the medical clinic, or some guard's podium that was unattended, tie it up, and attach a match head embedded in cotton as a fuse). Then smoking was banned and matches became unavailable. As they allowed us lighters back then, we could buy both lighter flints and fluid from the canteen, so it was common for someone to be sprayed with lighter fluid and set on fire. In the cells with open bar fronts, the rule of thumb was to sleep with your head away from the bars, in case someone decided to attack you. Then it would be your feet that got slashed or set on fire, rather than having your throat cut or face burned.

One of the most extreme cases of weapon-making happened at Folsom. A new warden was appointed to the prison, and he decided to add more metal detectors and more searches of inmates. But to show the new warden he didn't really control anything, one morning less than a month after he had added his new security measures, a five foot battleaxe was found with a sharpened three-leaf clover head, which is one of the patterns often seen in Aryan Brotherhood tattoos. It had been placed against the door of the Yard Sergeant's office.

Chapter 8

FOR A FEW CENTS MORE

It is blindingly obvious that very soon after entering prison, your mind has to turn to ways of acquiring the money necessary to obtain the items you need. The most obvious method is a job assignment.

Job assignments pay out a derisory amount per hour; the cleaners, porters and kitchen hands only get 12-15 cents an hour. Cooks and bakers might make 18 cents. Skilled trades, such as plumbers and electricians, would make 25-30 cents an hour and the clerks could make 30-50 cents an hour. If you were lucky enough to get into PIA (Prison Industry Authority), which made goods to sell on the outside, you could make from 30 cents up to 95 cents if you were good enough to get promoted.

Apart from the PIA jobs where you had to pass an interview, generally you were assigned to whatever job they chose to put you in, having little regard to what skill you might possess. If you did have a skill, it was up to you to make a personal approach to the supervisor of a function and beg for a job change.

No jobs paid very much, and as prisoners were supposed to work six hours a day, five days a week, apart from PIA which allowed you to work an eight-hour day, your 'take-home' pay was a pittance.

Not that we actually got 'take-home' pay, of course. The use of actual cash inside prison was strictly forbidden. I had not handled real money for more than 34 years when I came home, and getting used to using currency was yet another problem I had to face. Your earnings were credited to your personal 'trust fund', which held any money brought in with you or sent in from outside. When you go to shop at the canteen, or from an outside approved supplier, the money was deducted from your fund.

When most guys come into prison, they often don't have any money to bring with them. If they are lucky, they have family or friends on the outside to provide some financial support. An inmate becomes vulnerable by getting into debt with another prisoner. Prisoners will try to find a hustle that will get them things they need without having to 'borrow,' which is very risky and puts you in all kinds of dangers. The prison rule was that one inmate could not borrow, give or accept any personal property to or from another inmate, so perhaps selling wasn't included. But guards generally turned a blind eye in the belief that life was easier for them if you had something to occupy your time.

One of the easiest ways to acquire extra spending power was through your job. One of the most envied and powerful roles was that of housing clerk. He decided where new arrivals would be first housed but, more importantly, he was the person if you wanted to 'buy a cell'. Some wanted a cell far from the guard's station, so they could carry out illegal activities such as gambling, brewing pruno, sex, drugs etc.; others might want a cell that was closer to the beginning of their tier to make it quicker for them to get to the chow hall, yard and work line. There were even times when a guy would pay the person in a cell to move, and then pay the housing clerk to finalise it all.

The guys who worked in the kitchens could smuggle out food, or the maintenance crew could obtain materials, and then sell them on. There was very little that went to waste in the prison. Believe it or not, a fresh tomato could be sold for $1 and an onion, depending on its size, from $1-$2. Sandpaper, leftover paint or bits of wire also had an asking price.

For those who couldn't make a dime out of their

job, washing clothes for other inmates would often be the easiest thing to do. The prison provided the soap, water and buckets, and most guys hated to wash their personal clothes. You could not send clothes into the prison laundry for fear of them being nicked. Most guys would charge a soup, the 25-cent packet of ramen soup, for washing three pairs of socks or a tee shirt. Washing a pair of sweats cost $1 and jeans $2. Ironing was an easy hustle. Each unit usually had an iron and ironing board which an inmate could check out to use, so they could get their 'visiting' clothes looking nice. Ironing costs worked out at between $1-$2 an item, depending on how fancy the person wanted the creases done.

Sewing or repairing clothes often took a bit more skill to do it right if someone would be willing to pay you. You needed to be able to buy or barter for the needle and thread before you started, and you often needed to get a few different colours. This was one job I was able to do, as I had the skill from the streets. After doing the embroidery work on the jeans belonging to Sizzle, one of the queens I met at Vacaville, I had all the needles and thread colours I would need for years to come. I was actually able to make up and sell sewing kits to other inmates. A single sewing needle went for $5 and it would be 50 cents for a small wrapping of thread.

Those who knitted had to teach themselves how to do

it, as those who did know how didn't want any competition. You might think it funny, but there were a few
assaults on those found trying to cut into the action of
someone with an established clientele. At FSP, we had a
guy who would make all the characters from the Winnie
the Pooh stories. He was so good that the staff would
place orders. He was good enough to crochet names
onto the toys. It cost $30 – $100 per item, depending on
the size and model. There came a time when another
guy started to do the Pooh-themed characters to sell to
inmates and, yes, for less money. The first guy was so
insulted that somebody had dared to encroach on his
market that he got the second guy beaten up and paid
the assailants with a crocheted figure each. It was known
by the guards on the yard as 'The Winnie Attack'.

Other items that were crocheted or knitted were
beanies, gloves, scarves, socks, bed covers, cup cosies,
and bags. If they were made to order, they were often
made in the colours of a person's favourite sports team.
Some items were done in gang colours, or with gang
symbols for decoration, but once the guards realised
what they were, the item was confiscated. Inmates were
prepared to pay between $10-$50 for such items.

One of the more common hustles saw those who could
draw creating cards for holidays, birthdays, Mother's
Day or Valentine's Day. Those with the best skills, the

widest array of coloured pencils and who could provide the envelopes to send out the cards, received the best prices. Cards generally sold for $1 and up to $5 for unique ones. Those who could draw portraits could really make money and not only from inmates; staff would buy from them. Some sold for as much as $50.

There was a time when I put my hand to drawing portraits. I was a reasonably good artist, but not one of the best. Once, when I was at CMC, a guy approached me to do a family drawing of him, his wife and daughter. He gave me three individual photographs and wanted me to put them together into a nice family drawing. I explained I drew what I saw and was not one of the guys who made changes to the pictures. He agreed and I got to work. In the photo of his wife, I saw she had a large mole over one eye, his 14-year-old daughter was smiling but had no teeth, and he had a comb-over as his hair was quite thin. It took a couple of weeks to finish the drawing and chase the guy down for payment. When I gave it to him, he started to look it over and asked, 'Why is there a black thing over my wife's eyebrow?' I responded, 'Because it's in the photo you gave me,' to which he said that she was self-conscious about it. Then he asked, 'Why didn't you give my daughter some teeth?' I said, 'She doesn't have any in her photo' and he replied that it was because he couldn't afford to get her some. Lastly, he wanted to know why I didn't give him more hair. I said, 'Because you don't have any more hair.' He paid me what I had asked, which was $15 as I charged $5 per person, and he went away grumbling that he didn't think his wife would like it. Over the years, I would only do about a dozen portraits of other people. I generally used variations of myself in my works.

Wallets made out of old jeans or Naugahyde from furniture that had been thrown out were quite popular, even though we did not have any money, wallet-size photos or credit cards to carry in a wallet. We used them to carry our prison ID and privilege cards. Some guys who made these wallets would get quite inventive by painting designs or embroidering symbols, usually representing the person's gang, choice of motorcycle, car or sporting team. These would sell for between $10 and $35, with the highest price for one reaching $50.

Some of the more interesting hustles involved making boxes and picture frames out of rolled-up paper or folded cigarette packs. The rolled-up paper was often painted in a single background colour, then a couple of contrasting colours to try to give it a 'wow factor'. The guys who used the folded cigarette packs preferred either Camel, Marlboro or Lucky Strike packs as these gave them the opportunity to make patterns. Whenever the opportunity came to get coloured paper, such as blue, green, pink etc., they would happily use that. Other common items included baby booties and hearts with a person's name on. Most of the paper we used had to be purloined, and if you were caught with either pink paper or what was called goldenrod, you would be in trouble as they were the colours of the dockets, called chronos, that praised you. Obviously, in a prison there were foragers who could make them to order!

Over my 34 years inside, I had the opportunity to see how inventive and skilled so many people in prison really are. It saddened me that so many could do things that would have actually made them good money on the outside, yet inside they would trade away their efforts for just a bit of canteen, tobacco or drugs. Some guys did artwork that would easily have found a place in fine galleries, but would tell me that when on the streets they were too busy hanging out or partying to draw. Besides, their friends wouldn't think it was 'cool'. But anything anyone made as a hobby, if it was any good at all, had a value and could be sold for added income.

While I have written about being paid for goods or services, I do not mean it involved actual cash exchanges. Actual cash was not allowed. The nearest we came to that were $1 'ducats' that you could purchase from the canteen. The idea of ducats was that you could use them if you wanted to buy a self-portrait on the yard or from the visiting room, or to buy a soda, candy bars or ice cream from the mini canteen on the yard. The ducat was marked off in sections one through to 10, so if the item you bought cost 50 cents, they could take five sections and give you back the other five.

It stands to reason that the ducats were also frequently used as cash when bartering with another prisoner. And they were also used for gambling, which meant that it was possible to build up quite a stack if you were a successful businessman or gambler. But you were only supposed to be in possession of a maximum of 30 ducats at any one time. So, if you were unlucky enough to have a cell search at a time when you were affluent, you would lose them. The guards used them to pay informers on the yard, so they would stay in circulation.

Unfortunately, some inmates had very low paid jobs and absolutely no skills or talents to earn themselves a bit on the side. As they still needed to make some canteen, they often got roped in by one of the gangs, to carry drugs, tobacco, pruno, or smuggle in pornography or even weapons. They would never be given much and yet they also had to take any punishment meted out for possession if they were caught. This could include a referral to the district attorney, and could end up adding years to their original sentence.

Chapter 9

TIME ON YOUR HANDS

Chapels are another feature of all prisons. Most prisons had a chapel for the Catholics and another for the Protestant services. Within the Protestant chapel, it would often have a number of different denominations, such as Baptist, Methodist, Lutheran and Episcopal to name a few. There were two denominations which were not welcomed – the Jehovah Witnesses and Mormons. Along with all other religions, they were given the use of an inter-faith chapel. It was here that Muslim, Jewish, and Native American chaplains worked, and you could also find inmates who practised Taoism, Buddhism, Wicca, and Odinism. Even Satanists were allowed time for their worship needs.

Every inmate is assigned to a counsellor after being received at a prison or, in some cases, a particular housing unit. If you think these are people assigned to help, you would be completely wrong. They do nothing to counsel and, in fact, they only manage the inmates' prison file. Their main job was to report on an inmate's behaviour and programming, as well as making recommendations to the parole boards regarding the lifers. They were just ex-guards who were willing to take a small pay reduction for the privilege of wearing their personal clothes and being able to take weekends, holidays and nights off. Most of them only had a high school diploma.

Outside of work, eating and being on the yard, you are left with a lot of time on your hands. 'Doing time' was what us lifers thought we were doing, although we always told the short-term inmates that they were just 'killing time' until their release date. But whatever term you use, we had a lot of time to just stare at four blank walls, if we chose to. So most of us decided to do something else instead.

It will come as no surprise that watching mindless TV – soap operas and cop shows were the favourites – and listening to radio, especially on the yard or in the day room, were favourites. It was not unusual for a number of inmates to play different stations loudly and in competition with each other to the point where nobody could hear anything! Reading newspapers and books – sci-fi, fantasy, western and conspiracy theory genres were the most popular – were other ways to pass the time. The most common type of book in Ad Seg units were harlequin romances – in part it was to knock the guy's 'tough' image, and those kinds of books were also thought to have a calming effect. At a few prisons, there were even groups of prisoners so dedicated to the writings of David Icke that they had space for a study group in the inter-faith chapel, as they saw it as a type of spirituality.

It was also very common to see guys playing musical instruments, with guitars the most popular. But some had keyboards, saxophones, trumpets and harmonicas. Most prisons had a recreation department that arranged for bicycle races around the prison yard track. Cancer walks, health classes involving callisthenics, fixed fitness machines and music classes were part of the mix. The recreational department used to set up music and talent shows in the gym or on the yard.

The prison talent shows were, indeed, very talented. Inmates would showcase their talents, or lack of, to large gatherings. Attempts were made to entertain with poetry or readings, singing, telling jokes and, occasionally, doing an act from a play, which were often an inmate's original work. The shows always drew a good turnout, although usually a lot of heckling was involved.

At the first yard music show I saw in the gym at CMC, I was amazed at the quality and skills of many of the musicians. I could not believe how much talent was locked up behind the walls. I became friends with a guy known as Curly Ray. He was a country and western musician out of Bakersfield who, before prison, had played with Buck Owens and Porter Wagoner, two famous country western stars. Curly Ray was quite a character, drinking his coffee black and so strong a spoon would stand up in it. He also smoked about 20 hand-rolled cigarettes a day, but he played his guitar any time he wasn't at his job or in the chow hall. He often put together impromptu yard gigs, and always encouraged others trying to learn to play guitar. I never missed his shows and sang along, from the audience, to all the songs he played. His song list always included the prisoner favourites, *Folsom Prison Blues, San Quentin, Momma Tried, Green, Green Grass of Home, House of the Rising Sun, Wanted Dead or Alive, Wanted Man*, and many more. The songs of Waylon Jennings, Johnny Cash, Merle Haggard and Willie Nelson were always popular. And they would draw an audience of men of different races, which gave me a funny sense of hope in those few minutes of coming together.

I was at a gym show at CMC when Curly Ray, who must have heard me singing when I was part of his audience out in the yard, asked me to sing in his place as he had strained his voice and couldn't sing himself. Being the showman, his attitude was, 'the show must go on.' The last time I sang in public, apart from crowd singing, was when I was a child, so I had no experience of getting up on a stage and performing in front of several hundred men. But Curly Ray seemed to have confidence in me, so while he and the band played, without any prior rehearsal, I gave it my best shot, albeit nervously at first. The stage lighting was in my eyes, so I couldn't really see the audience, although I knew there must be 300 inmates and staff in front of me. I got through the first set of three songs and there was dead silence, which seemed to go on forever. Looking back, it must have been a stunned silence because nobody knew I could sing. But the next thing I heard was thunderous applause. Incredibly, I was a success! This was my first public performance, but not my last, as I sang for many groups over the last 20 years of my sentence, only stopping, or more correctly being made to stop, once I had been told I was an 'illegal alien'. Strangely, once I had stopped singing in public, I found, through my family history research, that my great, great grandfather had run a music hall, back in the 19th Century, my grandfather had been a professional singer in his younger days, and my father was active in amateur dramatics. My treading the boards must have been in my genes.

One of the best prison talent shows I ever saw was also at CMC, when a number of the queens got together and performed *It's Raining Men*. Their act included a chorus line of muscled-up guys, glistening with oil and wearing the shortest of shorts, gyrating behind the singers. The prison staff videoed the whole thing, and sent it out to be judged in a statewide competition, which they won. It was the first time I saw a complete standing ovation for an inmate performance.

Team sports were also part of prison life. There was quite a good softball team at CMC and local colleges would send in teams to play against the inmate team. Every time a college team turned up, the prison would field a team primarily of queens in very short shorts and tied-up tops, which would unsettle the very straight college boys. So much so, that CMC won nearly every game they played!

A more unusual pastime was playing marbles on the yard. That's right, grown men, convicted of violent crimes, would be down on their knees, shooting marbles into a circle drawn in the dirt, trying to knock their opponent's marble out of a divot in the centre. Some inmates got hold of 'steelies' as heavy shooters. These were just ball bearings, but served their purpose. I don't know why this game fell out of fashion, as players and onlookers alike would also bet on it. But even in 2017, when I paroled, some old-timers had hung on to a few of their marbles just for the memories.

Another activity that was very common was the role-playing game of 'Dungeons and Dragons'. I was always amazed how the players managed to get the different types of dice needed for the game. Some were made from wood or ceramics in the hobby shop, but the 20-sided die always came from outside. Because of my skills at woodcarving, I was often asked to make figures for the games. Not only did I make the warrior figures and the elves, dwarves and orcs, but I also made many of the monsters, and even ruins of houses or forts and graveyards to make the game more realistic, using only lolly sticks and small bits of rock and gravel from the yard.

Of all the ways we passed the time, the best was just sitting around with others and telling stories about criminal exploits, whether real or imagined or, as in some cases, even about the ones the guys planned to do once they were released. In part, this was how guys learned new 'skills' to use in crimes and also find new crime partners.

Chapter 10

STABBED OVER A GAME OF CARDS

Inmates often gambled, and I can't think of anything that someone wouldn't put a wager on. Both times I was found suitable for release by the parole board commissioners, there were bets placed on whether I would get approved by the governor, or if he would take it away (as he did with my first parole grant in 2013). Even guys on death row would have other inmates bet on whether they would get a reprieve. At prisons like Folsom and San Quentin, there were boards in the watch office that would record the number of beating, stabbings and deaths of inmates each month – and, yes, guards were not only known to bet on them, but it was found that guards made arrangements to hedge their bets by coercing inmates to up the score to what they needed to win.

Every card game – from pinochle, spades, poker, bridge and even ones like 'Go Fish' – were fair game. I witnessed a guy stab his own brother (a story I come back to later), who had been his partner in a pinochle game, because his brother had made an error in counting trumps, costing them the game and lots of money. He didn't die and they stayed cellmates.

It was the more highly-charged games like football, basketball, baseball (it did not matter if it was Little League, college or professional) and the Olympics that attracted the gamblers. Yes, even the Olympics, where there are lots of sports and countries to support. I have even seen guys betting on two praying mantises fighting. The most honest races in the betting pools were almost always either the Native Americans or the Pacific Islanders.

I remember one white guy at CMC who had an uncanny way of winning most of the betting pools. He had spent his entire life as a professional gambler and even bragged about being banned from some card rooms and at least one casino in Atlantic City, New Jersey and two in Las Vegas. The most talked about bet he won was when three guys bet him that he couldn't pick the winning team for the Super Bowl, before the season pre-games had even started. So, with nearly six months to the Super Bowl, he wrote down the name of the team, placed it in an envelope that was then sealed. All four of the inmates signed the envelope, as did staff who offered to secure it until it was time to open it. The day the game was played and the winner revealed, the envelope, which had not been tampered with, was opened – and he had named the team correctly. You should have heard the laughter from all those who had gathered to see the results, except the three who lost, as they had to pay out $50 each.

Sometimes the betting evolved into fights on the yard. It didn't matter if it was basketball, baseball, soccer or handball, if it was inmate players who were involved, you could be certain someone would accuse the other person or team of cheating, and then the fighting would start.

Watching the gamblers had its funny side, too. I recall watching a couple of guys at Deuel Vocational Institution (DVI) who were not only betting on the outcome of the chess match they were playing, but had decided to play 'Battle Chess' to make it more interesting. That meant every time a piece was taken, the person who lost it would get an open hand slap from the other guy. The guys playing had been drinking 'pruno' and had likely done drugs. I say that because they laughed like lunatics no matter what side of the slap they were on.

Board games such as Strategy, Risk and Monopoly

were also gambled on and this is how it was done when we had no cash. Poker is probably the easiest to describe. The basic bet would be 25 cents, the price of a Top Ramen soup. People would bring items they had purchased from the canteen or had received in their quarterly package. The items would be assessed by whoever was the banker for the game to the nearest quarter (25 cents). The banker would then issue homemade paper chits, worth 25 cents each, to bet with. At the end of the game, when it was time to cash in the chits, they would be exchanged for items to their value. Sometimes an IOU would be allowed, but usually there was a time period attached to that. They were given a few days or maybe a week to settle their debt. Non-payment of an IOU debt would be dealt with severely by the person who was owed the money. However, there was never a shortage of people who wanted to play and take the risk.

Chapter 11

HOME FROM HOME

As time passes, you find your cell is the place you retreat to. It provides some security and solace, and is the only place where you can sleep. It is often the place where you eat, and for much of the time it is where you exist while you are 'doing time'. But gradually, the cell becomes your identity and finally, at some point, sadly, you start referring to it as your 'house' or your home.

But there are other places that become important in your life. One of those is the mail room, where all the post is processed both in and out of the prison, not only for the inmates but all staff postings as well. It is only the inmates' letters that were opened and searched on the way in. Many prisons would even remove the stamps off the envelopes to prevent the drug LSD being on it or behind it. All inmates can expect their mail to be read, and if it arrives in a foreign language, it has to be translated first, which might take days or weeks.

All mail that inmates wanted to send out was placed in the housing unit's mail bag, which had to be left unsealed so the night guard on first watch from 10pm-6am could look at each envelope to ensure there was no contraband before sealing the envelopes. The guards are not supposed to read the letters, but that isn't always guaranteed if the night guard was bored. The only mail that would not be read was legal mail. This was the mail to either a court or an attorney, which the guard had to seal and sign, unread, in front of the inmate. I can say, sadly, that there were times when inmates did use this method to send out contraband, usually written information relating to gang business. However, there were times when guards would be given information that this was happening, and they would take control of the suspected envelope and have the appropriate legal specialist staff check it. Being caught misusing the legal mail system was serious and always brought charges and penalties to the inmate. But when one person abuses a system, harder rules are brought in and everyone suffers.

The mail room also delivered any magazines and news-papers the inmates ordered. You would be surprised by some of the publications inmates receive. Those who had a bit of money and invested in stocks and shares would have a regular order for the Wall Street

Journal. Some, who like to keep their cell looking good, would have home decorating magazines. Car and bike magazines were the most popular. Up until 1987-88, inmates used to work in the mail room to help process these periodicals. Unfortunately, due to abuse of that position by some inmates, it stopped. But the mail room is important to inmates as it is their connection with the outside world. If you get a letter in the post, the whole tier knows about it, and if there is some kind of go-slow or hold-up in the mail room, it affects everyone.

Then there is the package room, another important area for inmates. It is often attached to either the mail room or the receiving and releasing unit. It is from here that an inmate would pick up their quarterly package, which contains items they are allowed to order from a designated supplier every 13 weeks, or their special purchase such as a TV, radio or musical instrument. The package room was always run by a guard, and often by one of the 'strictly by the book' types.

Before the early 1990s, a better way to obtain privileges was to have a quarterly package sent in by a friend or family member. You were allowed one 30lb package each quarter, and though items were restricted, you could be mailed food, cosmetics, and certain clothing like blue jeans and a sweat suit. This all changed when companies started to become available for those inmates who had no one on the outside. An inmate could send money from their prison accounts and list the items they wanted from the companies' catalogues. The earliest of these companies were started by ex-correctional guards. The rules changed so that all quarterly packages had to be ordered through one of these approved vendors. Most state websites list who the prison suppliers are, and what can be bought and sent into prisons. Just as with canteen packages, it depended on your privilege group as to what you could get.

Those that were in 'A' group could purchase up to $140 a month, 'B' was $80 a month and 'C' $30. If you got in trouble, as well as losing good time credits, they would take away your canteen privileges. Given what we were generally served in the chow hall, the last thing you would want was to lose the opportunity to go to the canteen.

The canteen is just about the most important place in a prison as you can buy food items to supplement what you got from the chow hall. Of course, it was not like an ordinary shop. In your cell, you had a list of what they had for sale. On your designated canteen day, which was only once a month, you would take your wish-list to the canteen hatch, and wait patiently while your order was filled, which could take hours. No matter how much of your prison wages you had saved, the amount you could spend was based on your privilege group. Your privilege group was determined by your standard of behaviour; the better you behaved, the more privileges you had, which was reflected in how much you could spend in the canteen. By the time I left, the amount you could spend, depending on your behaviour, ranged from $30 up to $140 a month. Mind you, to be able to spend the highest amount you not only had to be near perfect, you had to have somebody on the outside sending in money as well, because there was nowhere in the prison that paid those kinds of wages.

The canteen is where you get your toothbrush, toothpaste, shampoo, soap, and that all important immersion heater or hotpot. The most popular items of food were the packet soups and noodles, instant refried beans, tuna, mackerel, sausages, mayonnaise, hot sauce, tortilla, corn chips, Ritz crackers, 'squeeze cheese' and the all-necessary coffee. If you had extra, then you might buy sweet biscuits, sweets, doughnuts, or a pint of ice cream. After receiving a rule violation, it was always canteen privileges that would be affected by either having the amount you could spend reduced or the privilege taken away for up to six months. This often caused severe consequences for an inmate who owed debts to other inmates, as they were mostly paid back in canteen funds.

Canteen price lists varied from prison to prison based on suppliers. There could be a big difference in the cost of items – which were generally more expensive than Walmart! However, there was one exception which stayed the same price at all prisons and was sold mostly to the prison population. That was the Top Ramen soup (dried noodle soup with a seasoning packet). These sold for 25 cents each and would often be bought by the case. The guys in 'C' group rarely had more than ten or twenty dollars to spend, so they would buy these soups, which were always the base ingredient in any 'spread' the inmates did with their group. Particularly when there were sporting events on TV, like football, baseball, boxing, etc… everyone would put in whatever they had – soups, maybe a can of meat or small sausage, a bag of dried refried beans, some mayonnaise – and after mixing it all together they might use tortilla chips as spoons, or if they were lucky someone would have tortilla wraps and they made burritos. Oh yes, we knew how to party!

Those that did have access to a regular flow of money would rarely go to the chow hall, opting instead to stay in their cell and eat what they could buy from the canteen and quarterly packages. I knew guys who had not been down for a chow hall meal in more than ten years. The canteen didn't sell healthier foods, but the food often tasted better.

Chapter 12

SECRETS OF PRISON TATTOOS

While in jail there is little to entertain people, so tattooing is quite common, though the ink and needles are harder to come by. So inmates have to become imaginative. For needles, they would use straightened-out staples taken from some legal paperwork, a paper clip or even a chicken bone smuggled back from chow. They would sharpen these up on the concrete floors and rinse them in either warm water, the hottest we ever got, or disinfectant we were given to mop the floor with. Cotton thread from a T-shirt would be wrapped around the needle to help hold ink. As for the ink, the simplest and most common method I saw was to take the paper sack that we got our lunch in, turn it upside down, set fire to a Styrofoam cup, and then collect the sooty smoke in the bag. It might take two to four cups to get the amount they wanted, which they would then scrape out into a plastic cap and mix with a bit of toothpaste and water. They would now have ink. It was very primitive, but in the right hands it served its purpose.

In prison, this skill is far greater and the artwork is much more involved than in county jails.

The common meanings of a number of tattoos used while I was in prison did slightly change, depending on which group had adopted it. Sometimes an individual would get a tattoo of what they thought looked 'cool', only to be approached by a prison faction and told to cover it up, or join them. In some cases, they would be smashed and it would be cut off their body. Many were pressured to get tattoos, while others were simply bored. Guys who couldn't afford tattoos would allow themselves to be used as a practice pad by someone trying to learn. Though they got a free tattoo, it was almost always terrible looking and if there was lettering involved, you can be sure there were misspellings. Around mid-2012, I started seeing more guys having their faces tattooed, in some cases to help them look tougher, especially if they had a baby face. Some said it was to ensure they would not be able to get a job when they got out, in the hope that the State welfare system would give them money for being unemployable.

I used to advise guys who were thinking of getting

a tattoo to really think about it, and not just because of the political problems that could arise. The California Department of Corrections and Rehabilitation reported nearly 20 per cent of inmates contracted Hepatitis C, HIV or AIDS – or, sadly, a possibility of more than one of these, so was it really worth the risk?

At Avenal State Prison, I was asked to spell out 'Peckerwood' in Irish Gaelic for a guy who said he had some Irish blood and wanted a tattoo to honour his heritage. I didn't really like the idea. Try as I might, I could not find anything in Gaelic for the word 'pecker', though the word for wood is 'Coll'. I went with what I believed (or maybe not) was the closest and gave him 'Bodcoll'. Without so much as a thank you, he just went off to have it tattooed across his back in Old English lettering. A few days later, a couple of guys who knew I didn't care for gang mentality, especially the 'white supremacist' type, asked me what it really said. As I couldn't find a word for pecker, I chose the word 'penis', which is Bod. In fact, Bodcoll actually means 'Peniswood'. The guy I gave it to was transferred. Then a few years later, on a yard at a completely different prison, a couple of guys were proudly showing off their 'Bodcoll' tattoos.

Teardrops: If the teardrop is just an outline, it symbolises an attempted murder. If it has been coloured in, it means they committed a murder. Within some gangs, a different side of the face symbolises a murder on the streets, or in prison. I have seen guys with three or four drops, as if to keep count. On rare occasions, a string of teardrops, going down someone's cheek, indicates the loss of a family member.

Cobweb: Usually represents a long-term prison sentence, and is most commonly found on the elbows and/or the neck. Alternatively, you might see someone with hinges on the elbows and backs of their knees. Sometimes, these would be done to look rusted, and for humour a small oil can would be tattooed next to them.

Three Dots: Usually found near the corner of the eye or on the web between thumb and forefinger on hand, meaning 'Mi Vida Loca' / 'My Crazy Life'. Five dots, with four dots surrounding the fifth, represent the prison walls, with the one dot in the centre being the person themselves.

1488: This tattoo has two separate meanings, used by mainly white prisoners. The first part (14) is from a Nazi leader named David Lane who came up with 14 words to express his ideology: 'We must secure the existence of our people and a future for white children'. The 88 represents the eighth letter of the alphabet, which is 'H', and when doubled up it means, 'Heil Hitler'.

Clover Leaf: The three-leaf is very popular for those in the Aryan Brotherhood, and anyone who gets this tattoo without their expressed permission is asking for trouble.

666: This is often used, not by those who might claim to be Satanists, but instead for shock factor, most generally tattooed on the forehead, face, neck and hands.

Our Lady of Guadalupe / Virgin Mary: Very common with Hispanic inmates, especially those from Mexico, Central and South America. Most often placed on their chest, often surrounded by a rosary. Some younger guys covered their whole backs with this tattoo as a way to deter the possibility of being raped, which was more common within the Hispanic population than other races.

Clock with no hands: Originally worn by guys with 20 years or more to serve. However, it had dropped from popularity until guys started coming in with sentences of 80 years all the way up to 1,000 years. As they were not technically 'Lifers', they would never go to a parole hearing, and so the hands had fallen off their life clocks.

Tombstones: Bricks in a crumbling wall will be used for a guy to mark off his years in prison, as they will put the year on it, such as 95, 96, 97, and so on.

Playing Cards: Often used to mean the person liked to gamble. However, when it is Aces and Eights (the hand Wild Bill Hickok was said to be holding when he was killed), it was most often a person doing life without parole, so a living death sentence.

EWMN: This stands for evil, wicked, mean and nasty.

Lightning Bolts and Swastikas: Most commonly found on white supremacist inmates, though it's not entirely unusual to see a swastika on a Native American, as they used it in their culture long before the white man came to America. It was customary for the whites to prove they had 'earned' their bolts by carrying out some action sanctioned by the gang.

Dice: This symbol is in pairs to symbolise a risk-taker. However, if the dice displayed aces/snake-eyes, the person sees themselves as a complete loser. Strangely, within the prison system a loser is seen as being bad luck and other inmates will avoid them. When a single die is worn, the other die is tattooed on a girlfriend or wife.

Skull: The person is surprisingly expressing optimism about overcoming obstacles. Skulls with flying hair represent the person's acceptance of death.

Clown Faces: Generally tattooed as a pair with one smiling and one frowning, meaning 'Smile Now, Cry Later'. This represents a belief in living life as recklessly as they can with little worry of going to prison, or death. These faces are inspired by Greek theatre masks representing comedy and tragedy.

Bullet Holes: Thought to be good luck or protective charms if tattooed on the chest. Drawn from the Native American warriors who wore 'Ghost Shirts', which were white deer skin shirts with blue spots painted on them, said to allow bullets to pass through without causing the wearer any harm. Tattooed bullet holes on the head signifies a plan to hold 'Courts in the Streets', meaning they plan to have a shoot-out with the police in which they will be killed.

Guns on Hips: Often this tattoo is a show of support for the Constitutional right to 'Bear Arms'. Among gang members, it was a way of telling others on the streets they were packing a piece, in an attempt to intimidate others. The most realistic tattoos looked like a gun in their waistbands, and police didn't take a chance when it looked as if the person's hand was a bit too close to it. Some have been shot, and a few have died, so you have to wonder if this one was a good choice for some ink.

Back Arms: This area is where most guys want to make a statement. Those in prison tended to tattoo things like 'White Pride', 'White Power', 'Brown Pride', 'Black Pride', 'Asian Pride' as well as 'Irish Pride' and 'Solid Wood', with one word on each arm. For me, in 1978, I chose to have 'Manx Bred' put on my back arms, which was a constant source of confusion for inmates and staff, while being an amusement for me. As far as bikers in prison went, you would often see on their back arms or backs, the name of their club, such as 'Hells Angels', 'Gypsy Jokers', 'Vagos', 'Outlaws', etc. Though a few might put things like 'Shovelhead', or 'Panhead', denoting the type of motorcycle they preferred. The funniest thing I have ever seen on the back arms of a white guy were the words 'Balsa Wood' as he would always be the first one out for a fight, but he only weighed 110 pounds, and even though he was six feet tall, the first punch to the head always knocked him out.

Many tattoos seen in prison yards about 10 years ago are starting to show up in mainstream society. The two most common were barbed wire and chains.

Chapter 13

LOCK-UPS, LOCKDOWNS AND 9/11

Lock-up, or more correctly 'Count Time', is a daily occurrence, six times a day. At every prison in California, there are regulated times at which all inmates must be accounted for, no matter where they are. At no time is a prison supposed to lose an inmate or gain one, without Sacramento headquarters knowing, as all counts are cleared there. At specific times of the day, an inmate locked in their cell or at a job assignment, medical appointment or at an activity like hobby shop, would be required to assemble in a place to allow staff to accurately count them. The times were midnight, 2.30am, 4.30am, noon, 5pm and 10pm. With the exception of being in Ad Seg, on suicide watch or on lockdown, these were the only times we were counted.

Back in the 1990s at one of the prisons near the Mexican border, their minimum-security yard only had a three-foot white picket fence as the designated perimeter. At an unexpected 10am count, it turned out they had more than 30 extra inmates. Illegal immigrants from Mexico were sneaking in, stealing prison clothes from the Hispanic inmates, getting some sleep on the bunks, a shower, and then taking breakfast and a lunch bag before continuing their trip into the US. The prison had noticed they had a substantial rise in the number of breakfasts and lunch bags they had been issuing for nearly six months. This issue caused an uproar in Sacramento HQ and caused the loss of rank of many senior staff members. This became the first minimum security prison to install double rows of razor wire-topped fences.

Lockdowns are the system's default position whenever there is a disruption in the normal running of the prison. This can happen when there is a riot, an inmate found dead, civil unrest outside the prison, earthquakes, severe storms that knock out power and yes, even war. Your cell door would be locked, and you would be stuck inside until at some point in the unforeseeable future the lockdown was ended. The only exception was that you would be allowed to go to the showers every three days or so, and if you didn't have the luxury of a water closet in your cell, you would have to attract a guard's attention to give you permission to walk along your landing to the toilet. Your three meals a day were delivered to your cell, by regulation, two being served up as 'paper bag' meals, and the third being a hot meal served on a paper plate, but often you would get three cold, bag meals instead.

Lockdown Boxes – It did not take long to realise it was common sense to provide yourself with a box which you kept under your bunk and contained the items you may need to better manage a lockdown, if only to supplement the food you were given. Most guys would keep packs of dry soup and noodles, jars of coffee, tea bags, instant dry refried beans, crackers, cookies, hard candy and packs of tuna. These were never touched, except during lockdowns or if you were rotating the use-by dates. Apart from 14 years when I was in dorm facilities and wasn't allowed to have one, the lockdown box was always a part of my life. It is strange that now I am free, the Covid pandemic meant I've experienced lockdown again. Was I better mentally prepared due to my experiences? I hope so.

One of the more dramatic lockdowns I experienced, though not the longest, was when four planes were hijacked in the US on September 11, 2001. I had just turned on my TV moments after the first plane hit one of the World Trade Centre towers, and then watched as the second plane came in as well. My first thought was there was no way this was some kind of fluke accident. The alarm went off throughout my housing unit, followed by the frantic announcement that 'the prison is now on lockdown; all inmates report back to their cells immediately'. Within minutes, you could not only hear the last of the porters who had been out cleaning being locked back up, but looking out of the cell doors, there were guards in full riot gear, some even possessing shields. The most distressing sight was that those who did not have shields were carrying large cannisters of pepper spray. As we had little in the way of ventilation, if they had fired that spray into a cell, it would have caused serious breathing problems for those inside. It was also discovered they had turned off the water to all the cells, which meant you would have had no way in which to get relief from the burning and suffocating spray.

Over the next couple of hours we would learn that two more planes that had been hijacked had been brought down, one crashing into the Pentagon and the other into a field as passengers had attempted to stop the hijackers from reaching their target, reported to be The White House. Inmates were calling out to each other that America had been attacked, and it had been by Muslims. This would have been disconcerting for the two Muslims who lived on my tier, as well as the others housed throughout the California prison system. You could hear mostly white inmates threatening to stab any Muslim inmate who went to the yard after the lockdown and, surprisingly, when the guards passed out sack meals while we were trapped in our cells, no Muslim got fed for the next two days.

Four days into the lockdown, a white guard offered those who were American citizens a sticker of the Stars and Stripes to stick to their cell door. Some inmates were allowed out of their cells for short periods to do their jobs such as porters for cleaning the unit, kitchen workers who were needed to fix trays for cell feeding, and a few clerks to work in the Watch Office. All of these inmates had the stickers on their doors and were non-Muslims. The lockdown lasted approximately three weeks.

Some Muslim inmates had chosen to lock-up for protection, though a few who, although they stayed on the line, kept a low profile. One of the biggest fears that ran through the inmate population at a number of higher-level custody prisons was that this incident may have led to some kind of civil unrest in the streets of America.

It was well known that the wardens at all prisons had a contingency plan for similar situations which might cause inmates to become disruptive and unmanageable. At Folsom and San Quentin, the standing orders were, if necessary, that during times of national security dealing with disasters, unrest or war, the guards were to be issued with rifles and go down each tier killing the inmates in each cell. Thankfully, it did not get to that point and I have spoken to guards who said they would not have followed that order, as they could not have lived with the consequences.

The longest lockdown I experienced was at Deuel Vocational Institution. It lasted almost 18 months and followed a series of incidents that had to be investigated individually. Initially, it started when the authorities attempted to return the majority of the housing units back to level 3 inmates after being reception units. Many of the level 3 inmates who arrived were unhappy that there was no political order at DVI at this time. The main line at the prison consisted of about 300 prisoners, who were the permanent inmate work crew. There were no gangs and no shot callers. Fights started almost immediately as the level 3 inmates jockeyed for position and attempted to carve out their own territory in the yard. There were a few assaults and a number of stabbings that started the lockdown. I was one of the lucky ones that still got out of my cell for a few hours each day during the week as I worked for the mental health department which processed all new arrivals. It was my job to set up the files for the psychologists to review and write their reports in. There were about 30 of us 'old' lifers who the staff knew and required our skills to run certain parts of the prison – medical, maintenance and warehouse.

However, every time the prison administration started to review the lockdown status and they let the level 3 inmates from different races out for a 'test run', there would be violence and the lockdown would be immediately re-instated. These reviews were carried out every 30-60 days. The level 3 inmates DVI received had been the 'problem children' that other prisons wanted to get rid of. To add to this chaos and confusion, there had been a major influx of sensitive needs prisoners (protective custody prisoners) into the reception units, who clashed with those who would become main-line inmates once they had been classified.

Why the prison staff at DVI thought it would be a good idea to house opposing groups of inmates together is beyond me, as immediately three reception inmates who had been categorised as sensitive needs were stabbed to death in their cells by their cellies. It was widely known on the main line that some level 3 inmates had been shouting over to the reception side, giving instruction that sensitive needs inmates needed to be 'dealt with'. It was these incidents and this extended lockdown that gave rise to a number of sensitive need gangs being formed at DVI, which then retaliated against the other reception inmates, causing the DVI administration into a major reshuffling of units to try to separate these groups.

What finally brought us out of lockdown was when the main shot callers of the whites and the Hispanics, as well as their lieutenants, were identified and transferred out to higher level institutions with the tag placed in their C-files of being members of disruptive groups. Though it did not stop all the politics, it did curtail it to a reasonably manageable state, which allowed the inmates, particularly those that wanted to go home, such as the lifers, the opportunity to feel they would not have to get involved in any of the stupidity that had gone on before.

Chapter 14

IN SICKNESS AND HEALTH

The medical care inmates received largely depended on the prison and if you could afford the $5 charge for all visits to the medical unit, except emergencies. This charge also applied to dental care, although rarely could you get a filling or a crown. It was standard practice to pull any problem teeth, which resulted in many inmates losing most of their teeth. If you did not have the $5, the staff had you sign a trust withdrawal slip, meaning as soon as you did receive any money, they would take it. They would even take it out of the inmate's 'Gate Money', the $200 they were given when they left prison to help them re-enter society. For some, it meant they may not get any gate money upon release. When you think about the fact that most inmates earned less than 30 cents an hour, often a guy would need to be seriously ill or even wait until he became a medical emergency if he could not afford the charge.

Valley Fever and other infections – The spreading of any disease was always of great concern, with the three most likely being HIV, Hepatitis B and C, as well as tuberculosis. HIV would be contracted either by illegal sexual activity, tattooing or intravenous drug use. Inmates would be most susceptible to Hepatitis B when working in the kitchens, clothing rooms and particularly the laundries. The California Department of Corrections was surprisingly on top of Hepatitis B by providing preventative inoculations, along with boosters recommended by the State Health Department.

In the first ten years I was in prison, every inmate would be tested for tuberculosis (TB) when they first arrived at the Reception Facility and then again whenever they transferred to a new prison. The CDC would also do a yearly testing of all inmates in their custody. In the mid-1990s, new arrivals were only sporadically tested and anyone infected would only be found out after yearly statewide TB checks. TB in the mid-1990s to early 2000 became an issue. There was a problem of it spreading as inmates had a habit of smoking off the same cigarette and drinking out of the same cups of coffee, as well as often using the same spoons when sharing a soup. Whenever an infected inmate was discovered, their housing unit would go on a mandatory lockdown until all the inmates living there could be checked for infection. In severe cases, a person infected with TB might be isolated in an Ad Seg cell rather than a hospital. This may be seen as a punitive action, but the main concern for the institution was trying to prevent extremely ill patients from becoming infected.

The biggest problem within the San Joaquin Valley prisons was a condition known as Valley Fever, a fungal infection that comes from the soil within the valley. Although it is not contagious, it can become chronic and, in some cases, has helped to contribute to the deaths of inmates who had suffered from immune deficiency illness or respiratory difficulties. One important factor was if a person had lived in the San Joaquin Valley, covering the area from Bakersfield north to Stockton, for more than one farming season, it is more than likely they will carry the spores that cause Valley Fever. I grew up in the San Joaquin Valley, and I was exposed, but so far it has not affected my day-to-day living. Valley Fever is known to cause what some people call 'Desert Rheumatism' and can include a combination of fever, joint pain, muscle pain, headaches, rashes, extreme fatigue or tiredness and, worst of all, a cough. The California prisons that showed the highest cases of inmates contracting this condition were Wasco State Prison, Avenal State Prison, Pleasant Valley State Prison and Corcoran State Prison. Within the inmate population, it is more likely for males rather than the females to contract more serious symptoms. Though it is a greater risk to some ethnic populations than others, it has been shown that the Filipino and African-American population will often have the severest symptoms, particularly if they were also susceptible to sickle cell anaemia. Age would also affect the severity of the condition, with more than one third of the deaths being in the 60 and over age range.

In 2010, California Department of Corrections started making mass moves of whites and Hispanic inmates down to the infected prisons from non-infected prisons, so blacks could have safer areas to live. Of course, should they develop health conditions that might weaken their immune system, it is possible this exposure could cause complications in the future.

Another big health problem was the spreading of flu and particularly the more dangerous Norovirus, which would often sweep not only through units of the inmate population but quite frequently the guards and staff working around the inmates, who then would take the virus back out to their families and communities. It was not unusual for staff shortages to happen during these epidemics, which would cause even more of a problem, as inmates who were not infected would find themselves either locked down or having their programme greatly reduced. Though it rarely happened, some inmates died from norovirus complications.

I contracted Norovirus my first year at DVI and I thought that I was the first in my unit to have it. I went to the medical clinic and reported myself, even though I knew it meant I would be quarantined. To me, it was the right thing to do, and I felt I was looking out for all the other inmates and staff in my unit. Both me and my celly, Samuel, were quarantined, and though he didn't like it, he did say I was far more considerate than most would be. We were moved out of L-3 and put down in C-Wing into a dirty cell with a couple of broken windows. The only light in the cell was hanging precariously from the electrical wires. As the light was above the upper bunk, it was Samuel who found out that if he wasn't careful, he would get shocked by the wiring when he sat up. Our quarantine time was 14 days, which, with Samuel suffering from Asperger's, was going to seem like a lot longer. He did not do well when he was not able to get out and walk around to relieve his stress and as he was not showing any symptoms, I was able to get one of the guards to allow him to walk on the back of the tier. During one of his walks outside the cell, one of the C-wing porters informed him all of L3 was in quarantine, after three other guys sick with Norovirus hadn't been responsible enough to self-report, despite feeling ill before me.

Samuel and I were stuck in the grungy little cell in C Wing for a couple more weeks as we weren't allowed to go back to L3, so as not to get re-infected. The worst part was that we had not been allowed to bring down any of our property. We had no books, no radio, no TV and certainly no food other than what was being provided. By the time we were reunited with our cell back in L3, I was a bit miffed by the other irresponsible inmates. I pulled the three guys up, who had been ill before me, and in front of a good portion of the guys in the unit I explained my dissatisfaction with them and told them very bluntly that if, in the future, I ever caught the plague I would be sure to come and infect them, and we would all die. To which they were very surprised and very apologetic about their selfishness and their lack of concern for the rest of us.

Chapter 15

CHRONO HOUNDS

Outside of work, hobbies and pastimes were not the only way of killing time in a California Prison. For those who seriously wanted to improve their life after prison, there was the hope that vocational training might give them a start in a new career, but for those of us who were lifers and had to depend on the whims of the parole board, it was the self-help classes that were the most important, even if they were entirely inappropriate to your circumstances.

There are a great many different courses, some that are a fad with the parole boards, while others are old standards like Alcoholics Anonymous and Narcotics Anonymous. Many of the courses have gone through changes, though the actual substance always seemed to stay the same. Courses can be as short as a few hours to intense programmes lasting years.

When I first got to San Quentin in 1985, the talk

of the yard was, 'Transcendental Meditation' which, as the prison is relatively close to San Francisco and an area that is generally seen as free thinking, there was a lot of support for inmate programmes by that community. It was strongly believed that if inmates could learn to do meditation, it would make them calmer and therefore easier to control by the staff. Of course, that would mean when they returned to society, they would hopefully no longer be the angry, violent, and selfish individuals they were when they went to prison, creating a win-win situation for all. This programme had been left over from the days of the hippies in Haight-Ashbury, that re-emerged with the 'New Agers' and the different progressive Christian churches that were starting to use crystals and rock bands to draw in new members.

Alcoholics Anonymous (AA) and Narcotics Anonymous (NA) are by far the staple requirement for most parole board panels when they are considering someone for possible parole. It did not matter whether a person had an alcohol or drug problem, part of the parole board's belief is that even if you didn't have an addiction, it was quite likely you would develop one when you got out of prison and had to cope with the shock of re-entry into society some 25-plus years later. So, in their minds, they were trying to help. It would often vex them when someone didn't take one of those programmes. When they questioned me about it, it was as if they believed that if I rode motorcycles, I had to be drinking or taking drugs. I kept trying to explain that being impaired by drink or drugs was not conducive to riding motorcycles and not being killed, but they could never get their heads round that concept.

I knew hundreds of guys who would not only participate in the AA and NA programmes, but often became the guys who ran the meetings (to get the best chronos for the parole board, only to at some point years into their sobriety suddenly 'fall off the wagon' by drinking illicit pruno, which would wreak hell from the next parole panel they appeared before. They would be seen as hypocrites by others in the programmes, when the truth was, it was at these very programmes where illicit drugs were often distributed. The parole process started the year after an eligible inmate started in prison, with a 'Documentary Hearing', where a single member of the parole board evaluated what you had done with your time and suggest things that might be more suitable for release when you appeared before a full parole panel.

At my Documentary Hearing, I was told to take an AA course, after I had made the mistake of mentioning to the board member that, although I was not a drinker, on one occasion in my entire life, after a divorce judge had taken away access to my son, I had got drunk.

The suggestion I should take AA was seen so positively by parole panel members and though I protested my non-use of illegal substances, it seemed if I was to get home at the earliest opportunity, I would need to do this. I did nearly two years of AA at CMC, but as there were so many people on the waiting list to get help that really needed it, the staff sponsor asked that I give up my seat, as I had no history in or out of prison dealing with either drugs or alcohol. But at least I got the slip of paper, called a chrono, which proved I had done as I was asked. Years later when I was asked by parole panel members, I would show them the chrono, and though they were not happy, they had to accept the fact I had met my obligation.

Some self-help programmes were done by mail, such as the Criminon Courses (provided by a branch of the Church of Scientology) which were highly respected in the 1990s by the parole board. As an example, I will give you a list of the ones I took to try and show the parole board that, if given the chance, I would re-enter society as a better, more understanding man.

Those inmates who took every course they could were generally referred to as being 'Chrono Hounds' by parole board panel members, as they saw these guys as trying to impress them and possibly attempting to manipulate a date of release. It was far better to take a reasonable number of classes spread over time, while also participating in other positive programmes, such as hobbies, music, sports, writing classes and, if possible, even talent shows, usually sponsored by the prison coach or education staff. I involved myself in a variety of things, which I believe made my time go by smoother. I did not start any self-help programmes until after I got to CMC in 1986, as the previous prisons were too unstable to get involved.

Starting in 1987, I embarked on trying to do one self-help course a year, and each one would take anywhere from 90 days to 180 days to complete. While I was at CMC from 1986 through to 1993, besides the two years of AA, I also took Anger Management, Domestic Violence, Oral Communication, Rational Behaviour and Good Decision Making. As most were pretty straight forward, I rarely spoke up in the classes (which had about 15-20 guys). For Rational Behaviour, I felt as though I had to, as this programme wanted to teach us how we were to keep calm in all situations. I gave the example of when you are confronted by a guard and if you are calm, it will only exacerbate the contact, as the guard will think you are being a smart-arse. The next thing you know, you will have half a dozen guards all standing around yelling at you. So I merely stated that if the guards didn't put into use Rational Behaviour, it was a futile effort on the part of the inmate to calm the situation.

I was moved through four prisons between 1993 and 1999 and, due to a surge of inmates going into the protective custody units, many prisons were having to convert some yards to accommodate these changes. So, though I did get some vocational training, I was only able to take the following self-help classes: I-See-Hope, Opportunities for Personal Enrichment, Personal Responsibility & Controlling Anger, Conflict Resolution & Stress Management.

Once I got back to Folsom in 1990 until 2005, I was able to get into a few more courses: Personal Health Assessment and Self-Energising System (P.H.A.S.E.S), Respect & Responsibility, Defusing Violence, Family & Community Care. I also completed 19 FEMA (Federal Emergency Management Administration) courses, which were seen as both educational and self-help, as they were training to support a community in case of a tragedy.

A Guide to a Meaningful and Responsible Parole
− This class, offered in 2003, was not actually a self-help class, though it was run by a psychologist and

psych tech at Folsom State Prison. This class was for those inmates who had taken dozens of courses previously, and it was hoped if they saw the opportunities available when they got out, it would provide hope to do better in prison. Most of the inmates had to go before a parole board panel to be found suitable, and the panel wanted you to have skills for employment. A Dr. H Shrum, one of the more senior psychologists, came up with a seven-page 'Re-Entry Resource Booklet', which answered a number of inmates' frequently asked questions. It included places that would hire ex-felons, how to best present yourself to a prospective employer, and what kind of attitude you needed to have in a workplace. The booklet contained a section for anyone going before a parole panel to use if challenged about job skills.

**RE-ENTRY RESOURCE
BOOKLET ADDENDUM**
A Guide to a Meaningful and Responsible Parole
Dr. H. Shrum / Ms A. Carte
Re-Entry Coordinators
2003 Edition
Folsom State Prison Education Annex
P.O. Box 71
Represa, CA 95671

CONTENTS

Here is what they suggested using at a parole board hearing.

Have No Skills? Think Again!
Skills learned in crime can be applied well to skills required for legitimate pursuits. For example:
Murder/Manslaughter/Assault: Strong confidence level, not afraid to speak up or ask questions; self-moti-

vated, not easily intimidated, not bothered by stress; can be counted on to get the job done.

Hustling (drugs, services, goods, etc.): Good ability to sell, keen marketing sense; not easily disappointed; can talk to people of different ages, backgrounds & educational levels; know how to close a deal.

Prostitution: Works well independently or in a team situation: can follow directions; not afraid of hard work; creative, proven sales ability; outgoing personality; skilled in customer service.

Embezzlement: Excellent accounting skills: patient; well organised; detail-oriented; professional demeanour, hands-on computer experience; goal setter; works well with little supervision.

So, you tell me, if you were reviewing someone for release back out into society and they came before you and listed off their skill set based on this booklet – would you let them go free?

Once I was settled back at DVI in 2005, where I would be for the next 12 and a half years, I had the opportunity to be involved with a wide array of self-help programmes, as they were constantly starting new ones.

Digging into Yourself – This was a special programme that started at DVI shortly after I arrived in 2005 and because it was run by the senior psychologist, Dr. S. – everyone on L-3 wanted to take it. The presumption was that to receive a chrono signed by him would carry more weight at a parole hearing. For the record, senior psychologists did not normally do any personal interactions with inmates and certainly did not actively participate in a self-help class. But Dr. S. was a bit different. Even some staff referred to him as 'Dr. Shermhead', not because he used drugs, but because he tended to be unconventional and even a bit forgetful at times. He was, however, well respected by the lifer population as he was known to stop in corridors and speak to them, checking in on their wellbeing.

As this class was only six inmates at a time, and many wanted to take it over and over – trying to collect as many chronos as they could – and with each class lasting eight weeks, there was a waiting list. It took me more than three years to get in. This class focused on a person really delving into themselves to try and not only see where they may have gone wrong in life, but what factors may have caused them to make the wrong decisions. Though this class did not allow someone to say 'I had bad parents' or 'I fell in with the wrong crowd', it was geared towards a person trying to understand that it is never about what happens to you, but what you do because of it, and finding better ways to respond.

In many ways, this class did offer up some good points, if a person actually took the time to apply them in their lives. This was not going to be practical for most of those who took it, though. Many were just chasing chronos trying to get as many 'Atta-Boys' as they could to hopefully impress the parole board panel. The final assignment for the class was to write your own obituary, to give an idea of what you hoped would be said about you once you had died. Many found this quite disturbing and hard to do, though you did have inmates trying to impress by writing what they thought Dr. S wanted to hear, such as 'He was a good father, loving husband, and a contributing member in the community'. Sadly when two or three in the class of six wrote in the same vein of thought, it doesn't have the same impact.

I went a different way as instead of my obituary, I chose to go with an epitaph. At this point, I was still trying to get the British government to accept me as a British citizen as, illegally, my own birth had not been registered, and I had learned more about how, though not why, I was sent away from the Isle of Man as a baby. I still had no idea if I would ever get out of prison and if I did, if I would ever get back to the United Kingdom. It had come to the point where I felt that I needed to make a strong statement. When I read the epitaph in front of the whole class, I could tell by the looks on their faces, including Dr. S, that this was far from what any of them expected. There were a few who, even though you weren't supposed to talk about what goes on in self-help classes, chose to tell others about what I had written, and I had some come to ask me about it, and to find out if that was how I really felt. I was surprised by the effect my words had on others. It was in part because of this speech, that when I lost my job at PIA, Dr. S offered me a job working with the staff in the psych department.

Epitaph of Morgan James Kane
He was born into a world that never knew him,
Lived in a world that cared not for him and
Died in a world that will not remember him.
He was a better man than many ever knew and
A worse man that some would have believed.
He tried his best, even though he never could save
Any of those who loved him.
So, he leaves this world as nothing more than a
Single breath of air…
One taken on his way in –
One given on his way out.
He who never was, is no more…

Then, in about 2006 or 2007, there came about a big change. Suddenly the 'new' thing all parole board panels wanted to see and hear about was 'Insight & Remorse'. This may seem reasonable, but how do you show someone something, if they are not really sure of what it looks like. Those two concepts are subjective terms, and it was often seen that where one panel member may think an inmate has shown neither, another member may say the inmate showed 'limited' examples of both. This creates conflict when a parole board psychologist has written in their assessment report that the inmate shows 'full understanding of insight into their crime and complete remorse for their actions'. This happened a number of times, where the board panel and the psychologist didn't agree, which would only add to the frustration when the hearing ended in a denial.

I have been caught up in this kind of cat and mouse game with parole boards. They never could accept you might have one without the other, and so it became part of the discussion in every self-help group. Inmates always want a fast way to give the board what they are asking for, just to get that elusive parole date. Most would have preferred if they could just be told exactly what to say to convince the parole board it was their time to go.

Did I ever convince the parole board panel that gave me my two dates? I don't think so. In fact, it would have been pretty difficult to have 'insight' into my crime, as I didn't actually commit it in the first place. As for remorse at the victim's death, by the time I went to the boards that found me suitable, I had irrefutable proof the victim was being paid to, and intended to, do me harm.

Other courses I took were: Stress Management, Victim's Awareness, Forgiveness, Communication, Exploring Boundaries, Problem-solving Through Discipline, Understanding & Handling Addiction, The Four Agreements, Stress From The Inside Out, Anger Management, The Quiet Mind, Science of Achievement, The Way to Happiness, Personal Integrity, Conflict Resolution, Life-2-Life, Anger & Stress Management, Handling Suppression, Partnership for Re-Entry, Life Experience, Learning Empathy, Memory Defence Mechanism, Taking Responsibility, Post-Incarceration Stress Disorder (PISD), Helping Each Other, Relapse Prevention, Forgiveness, Depression Awareness, Victim Impact, Learning from Adversity & Defeat, Self-Control & Self Discipline, Thinking & Feeling, The Purpose Driven Life, Helping Hands, and Taking Charge of your Life.

The last one I took was called GOGI.

GOGI, which meant 'Getting Out by Going In' was a year-long course, involving four 12-week modules, which required every participant to do rigorous introspection of and deep self-reflection in applying the 12 GOGI tools. Once a person had completed the year-long course, the outside instructors would encourage them to take extra training, so they could spread the teachings of GOGI to others, especially when they were transferred to other prisons. Personally, I saw this as a cult-like group, because of the intensity with which the instructors would force the teachings. A number of inmates had that weird glaze of the eyes and constantly spouted GOGI teachings like those who think they have found a Messiah, such as the Manson family or followers of Jim Jones and David Koresh. These inmates would become confused and even hostile if those they were talking to didn't take to the teachings.

Many people who find themselves in prison can often look back to the fact they were easily led by others and unfortunately, none of the self-help courses I ever took spoke about a person becoming more self-reliant. More often, they would say you need to follow what this book or person says, which I saw as being counterproductive.

Vocational Training / Certifications. As with self-help programmes, it was very important that all inmates who came before the parole board must have some employable skills to help ensure they would have a chance to find a job and lessen the chance of returning to crime. The number of training courses changed drastically over the years, in both the viability and the quality of the teaching. The idea that you as a prisoner, at whatever age you finally leave prison, will be able to walk into a job the moment you are free is something that you come to believe in. The reality is, of course, entirely different, but when you are inside, you don't know that.

When I first went to California Medical Facility (CMF) in Vacaville, they were training inmates for employment in the free world in courses such as Surgical Tech (two-year course), X-Ray Tech (five-year course), Lab Tech (two-year course) and Certified Nursing Assistant (one year). A good number who completed these courses did go out to work in these professions, though I will admit, not all were successful.

Up until around 1998, most institutions still had inmate X-Ray techs, as they were often lifers and to keep their certification, they had to complete so much training and actual work hours. Every one of them that I knew had hoped to continue working in that field when released. But then the prison system just did away with the position of inmate X-ray Tech, which for those who had done the five-year training programme and then had used those skills for 10 to 15 years, but were suddenly told they would need to take up a different skill set, it was devastating. Believe it or not, the parole board took the decision at this time that those people had no employable skills and many were given longer denials to allow them to pick another vocation and get trained before reappearing in front of a parole panel.

Though every prison had some vocational courses available, most were really sham courses – Landscaping and Janitorial were created so the prison had a free non-paid work force to keep the prison grounds and buildings clean and tidy. Courses in Auto Mechanics, Small Engine Repairs and Auto Body & Paint would be thought as good trades to learn, but were so out-dated that even if an inmate graduated at the very top of the class, he could not take his skills out of prison and get hired in a shop, simply because the equipment and techniques were so far behind the industry standard.

The California Department of Corrections & Rehabilitation, was not putting the money into the 'Rehabilitation' side of their title to make available any real programmes to help someone who wanted to make a change. From their standpoint, what is the benefit for them if people stopped committing crime and become law-abiding, tax-paying citizens? The prison system had gone from two prisons, nine men's institutions, two women's institutions and about 36,000 inmates when I first went to prison in 1984 to, by the time I was finally released in 2017, 33 state prisons and more than a dozen private ones, holding, at one point, more than

220,000 inmates. The prison system is a business and prisoners are its fuel and product, so if rehabilitation means empty beds, and empty facilities, this ultimately means fewer jobs and less revenue.

I would see small attempts at different prisons to try to update some vocational programmes. Unfortunately, one problem was that the staff hired to teach the courses didn't know the subject they were teaching. Many of the vocational instructors were ex-guards who had been injured (sometimes in the line of duty). That meant they could not be guards, but didn't qualify for retirement, so by teaching these courses they could continue on to get their full state retirement when they reached 20 years of service. After many of the courses, the inmates might never receive any manual jobs.

Plumbing, Electrical, Heating / Ventilation /Air Conditioning. These training courses were usually done through the prison's maintenance department and taught by the free staff. This training was generally really good, but the drawback was that no certifications were given out, which meant that the inmate would have no proof of training, though it would be in his C-File, which means if he returns to prison, he would find a job quickly.

At some prisons they had training programmes dealing with animals that could offer job skills in, for example, large-scale chicken and pig production. These programmes really benefited the paisa inmates, who had experience with this industry. The Prison Industry Authority (PIA) provided the programme as their whole purpose is to manufacture things for state institutions and agencies. They rented space within a prison to run their shops and provide work training and wages for the inmate workers.

High Desert State Prison – unusually, inmates trained mustang horses taken from the wild by the US Bureau of Land Management of Federal Lands and ran a horse adoption programme to the public.

Avenal State Prison – had a Furniture Factory, which made primarily wooden furniture, such as tables and desks. They had a **Mill & Cabinet** course, and I took that course, though for my own knowledge. They also had a **Metal Fabrication Shop** and outside the prison's electric fences were the chicken hatching, raising barns and abattoir. For a while they had both a pig and emu farm.

Folsom State Prison – had one of the older and most important PIA factories, the **Licence Plate Factory**, established in 1947. This is considered to be one of the best places to work, though historically it has been one of the more dangerous as well.

California Men's Colony – this had the most shops that I know of in the CDC / PIA system. Though Folsom made the metal licence plates, it was the CMC PIA Print Shop that manufactured the yearly registration stickers. There were also a Knitting Mill (for socks), Glove Factory, Jacket Line, T-Shirt Line, Silk-screening, Shoe Factory, Laundry, Warehouse and Maintenance Department.

There were also activities like a butcher shop, coffee grinding, and flag-making. I received training in all the skills needed to work in the following fields of employment – Industrial Laundries, Commercial Shoe Factories, Commercial & Domestic Janitorial, Offices Services, Powder Coat Painting, Industrial Maintenance, Brake Press Operator, Customer Service Specialist and recertified as a Motorcycle Mechanic.

Yet, even with all these job skills and the number of self-help programmes I participated in, there were times when I had parole board panel members look me in the eye and tell me I had 'programmed in a limited manner'. This caused me and many others to wonder what their real agenda was, as I have seen more than a few inmates, who never took a single self-help or vocational training course, go before a parole panel and not only be found suitable, but not even get reviewed by the Governor before waltzing straight back out to the streets.

Chapter 16

MY FIRST PRISON

It is common policy within the Californian prison system to move inmates every few years. The idea is to prevent an inmate forming a lasting friendship with another inmate, or becoming too familiar with any members of staff. Whether that works in practice, I cannot say, I just know that over my 34 years inside I was moved a total of 12 times, returning twice to three of the same prisons. On each return, it was like going back to a totally different place, because although the building stayed the same, the regime had changed.

Folsom State Prison

This was my first prison, and it was intimidating, being one of only two level 4 maximum facilities in California in 1984, the other being San Quentin. I was held here twice, adding up to almost 6½ years. What both level 4 prisons had in common was tall stone walls, guards with guns, both on the perimeter walls and in the cell blocks, and the gun walks which encircled the cells. These were places where mirth and merriment were never seen. The heavy cloak of despair, sadness and fear hung in the air. You could taste it. The weight could be seen on the shoulders of most inmates and staff. One of the main things that made Folsom stand out from San Quentin is that it was positioned in the remains of a granite quarry where you could find the stone, 'Folsom Black Granite', which was used to build the walls.

These walls are impressive when you drive up to them on a prison bus, and help give Folsom a truly awe-inspiring castle-like image. It is said they are not only 26 feet tall to prevent anyone scaling them, but also 26 feet deep, so you weren't likely to tunnel out either. When I worked up on China Hill, during my second time at Folsom, I would have the opportunity to get right up close to the wall and was amazed to find that inmates had carved their names and the dates they were there in some of the stones. These walls are about five feet thick and each of the stones weighed around 500-800 pounds. Yet every single stone was cut and shaped by convict blood, sweat and tears, using primarily hand tools. As it was built in the 1880s, not only were the walls built by convicts, but so was the rest of the prison, stone by stone. This was at a time when going to prison truly meant doing time and hard labour, something that no inmate in any western world prison today can even imagine.

I had the opportunity to read some of the old logbooks and see photographs of what life was like at Folsom from the 1880s-1930s, when I worked in the watch office as the Captain's Clerk. One that stuck in my mind was a photo taken in the 1920s, showing naked prisoners, chained together by their wrists, being led into the American River (which Folsom prison backs up to) to bathe. Yet the photo shows a good foot of snow on the ground. On the back of the photo, someone had written, 'prisoners take their once-a-month bath – whether they want it or not'. Can you even imagine that being done today? The bottom of the quarry site down by the river is nearly 150 feet below the top of the prison wall and surrounds most of the prison. Not all the stone quarried was used at the prison, as it was primarily being cut to be shipped out to be utilised in other building projects both in and out of the state of California.

I have always felt it was the cold and bleakness of those granite walls that led to the same cold, bleak demeanour in the majority of inmates and staff. It was as if the longer you were there, life was sucked out of you and some guards who had worked there 25-30 years were little more than shells of whom they may once have been. Except for two parts of the song *Folsom*

Prison Blues, every time I hear that song, I have flash-backs to events, feelings and even smells. I doubt I will ever lose the mark it made on me, though, unlike many others, I survived, got out and didn't let it define me.

There are two mistakes in the song. First, if you shot a man in Reno (in the state of Nevada), you would not go to Folsom Prison (in the state of California) and secondly, when Johnny Cash sang, 'I hear a train a comin, it's rollin around the bend' in the song, there were no trains passing anywhere near the prison. Once there had been a train when the granite was dug, cut and shipped. It had been a narrow-gauge railway that ran a couple of miles from the prison to a main line, where the granite would be loaded on to larger trains destined for building projects far and wide. When there was no use for the little narrow-gauge train, first the prison tried to sell it, but when no takers could be found, it was decided by the warden at Folsom just to have the engine backed up into a mining shaft. The opening of the tunnel was collapsed, sealing it in. Perimeter guards have gone down to the tunnel entrance and been able to take photos of the front of the engines. This is seen as a terrible end to a train that had done so much for the legacy of Folsom Prison, but when you think about all the men who died serving their time buried on the hill behind the prison, it is almost a memorial to them.

It said to most of us inmates, 'when you can no longer serve a purpose, you'll just be buried.'

Like the train, most of the dead inmates have no headstone, they were just laid to be forgotten. But those days are long gone. Inmates are no longer buried there or at any prison. If an inmate dies in prison and has no one to claim their body, as would have been the situation for me if I had died, then the state of California will just cremate the body and discard the ashes in some unknown location. The last person to be buried at Folsom was in the 1980s. He was known as the 'Folsom Flea' and died at the California Medical Facility – Vacaville, before being brought back to Folsom, having won a state court order allowing him to be buried there. He had served more than 50 years. He and his sister had been the last of the 'Highwaymen' type robbers in California back in the 1930s. His sister had died many years earlier, the story goes, but none could say if she was in prison when it happened.

When I first arrived in 1984, the place had an ominous feel about it, like a tomb. Initially, I was placed in #1 Building, which was five tiers high and held the largest population for a single building within the California corrections system. Although I was 30 years old when I entered Folsom State Prison, the average age on the yard was 22. It amazed me to learn that most of the guys I met actually thought prison was a good thing because they had friends in it. At this time the prison was, to a certain extent, self-supporting with a fully operating butcher shop and bakery.

Once a week, we would watch a refrigerated truck drive up to the West Gate and unload half-sides of cow carcasses onto the hooks connected to the conveyor belt that would take the meat inside the freezer area of the butcher shop. The free staff butcher would only hire inmates to work for him who were in prison for murder or assault, as he felt that they would be the least squeamish around blood. Though this job only paid eight cents an hour, the perk came from having the opportunity to eat the choicest cuts of meat. The best paying jobs were up on the Prison Industries Authorities (PIA) hill where the licence plate factory, the sheet metal factory, and the paint factory were all located. These jobs paid between 20 cents and 65 cents an hour, though you had to go through an extra security search, including being strip-searched twice a day – once on the way up and once on the way down.

The only other opportunity to do something positive with your day was to be assigned to either a vocational trade or to be placed in the education department. In my opinion, one of the most dangerous places to be was in the vocational auto shop. In the short period I was at

Folsom the first time round, five guys had been stabbed to death by other inmates, placed on dollies, rolled back under vehicles, which were then lowered down onto their chests. Most of these guys were killed over drug or gambling debts.

People have said many times that in prison 'life is cheap'. Even the slightest misunderstanding, or act of disrespect (real or imagined) could get you cut, if not killed. The most senseless killing I saw came about over a pack of Camel cigarettes. Packs of cigarettes were often the only real currency used in prison and though they might only cost 80 cents a pack, they were valued at $1 each. On the third tier in #3 Building lived a guy named Grubs, who was known to give out loans of cigarettes, though he charged interest. If you borrowed one pack, you had to pay back two packs. One guy who always dealt with Grubs and paid him back on time, suddenly had his canteen privileges revoked for six months due to a rule violation, so he couldn't pay back the debt. The interest that Grubs charged went up another pack for every week it wasn't paid. The guy could have borrowed the cigarettes from someone else, though if they knew how badly he needed them, they would charge him to pay back three or four packs for each one he borrowed. You can see how quickly a debt can get out of hand. It had been about six weeks that the guy hadn't paid Grubs back, but finally he was able to get two packs from somewhere and gave them to Grubs, but told him he wasn't paying any additional interest. He returned to his cell, six or seven cells down the tier from Grubs'. A couple of hours later, the guy came out of his cell wearing only boxer shorts, flip-flops and a towel over his shoulder, carrying his soap and shampoo, on his way down to the ground floor to take his daily shower. Just as he moved past Grubs' cell, Grubs stabbed the guy three or four times in the back, a couple of times in the chest and then hoisted his still breathing body up and over the safety railing on the tier and tossed him over. The fall from the third tier is about 35 feet and there were no safety nets. The guy landed on his head and was killed instantly. All due to a few packs of cigarettes and a show of disrespect, a man lost his life.

Many men who were desperate jumped from those tiers, some because they owed debts and feared they would be stabbed, some chased by others with knives. Then you had those who had lost all hope of either getting out, or they had received bad news – the death notice of a family member, usually their mother, would often be the tipping point. A few jumped because of a 'Dear John' letter. Those most intent on carrying out suicide would actually go up to the fifth tier in #1 Building to jump, the fall there being closer to 70 feet and nearly always fatal.

One of the few places considered safe and a sanctuary was the Greystone Chapel. All the gangs had a pact that no matter how badly they wanted to hurt someone, no one would be stabbed inside. At Greystone Chapel, on its wall above the altar, is a painting of the Last Supper, painted by an inmate. What wasn't realised by the staff at first was that all the disciples were actually based on convicted murderers he had known at Folsom. He then added his own special extra detail, which was his face painted into one of the folds of the tablecloth, looking up at Jesus.

Though I tended not to get involved in any sports outside of lifting weights, I was asked to sit in as a fourth in a pinochle card game. I knew how to play, but I wasn't very good as I had only learned in the county jail. This was the last game in the tournament and it was all coming down to one last hand I was going to be playing. Those who played regularly knew there was an expected order in which cards would be played. Since I didn't play regularly, I apparently played in such a manner that I threw off the member of the other team who was keeping the count of the trump suit and the secondary suit that would become trump in the game.

The two guys we were playing against were brothers and cellies who were known to win most tournaments. As our game progressed down to the final round of cards, I played the trump card, with a cheer from my partner and a look of shock and dismay on the faces of our two opponents. Suddenly, the brother who was not keeping count pulled out a knife and began stabbing his own brother in the left shoulder and upper part of his chest, all the while yelling 'You fucking dump-truck, you lost us the game.'

Luckily for his brother, the blade on the knife was only two inches long. The two brothers immediately headed to the shower behind Blood Alley to clean up the mess. It turned out not a single guard saw or heard the commotion, and later my card-playing partner informed me he had been paid the $150 pot by the brothers, as the winnings for the tournament. He gave me $30, but I chose not to play any more cards in prison as it seemed people took losing too seriously.

My first job at Folsom State Prison was as a surgical technician. This job gave me access to inmates' medical files, which provided the personal listings of home addresses to contact in case of emergency, and any injuries or medical conditions. All of this was more leverage to be exploited by the gangs when needed. I was one of four surgical techs; the other three were members or associates of prison gang factions, with one position each set aside for the AB, BGF, and the Eme. It was my skill as a Navy corpsman which qualified me to do the job, whereas the other three inmates received their training on the job. Each of us were assigned to a different doctor, but to help keep the peace the prison staff always tried to maintain a representation of all the main races – white, black and Hispanic – even though the staff knew they were likely involved with gangs.

I was allowed to do a number of minor surgery procedures. One was to remove birdshot (that had been fired by the guards out of shotguns, most often as a result of being in the middle of a fight between inmates). Birdshot was used as a deterrent and not meant to cause permanent or serious injury, with the rare chance that someone might be blinded if struck in the face. In the chow halls, usually a 'Block Gun' would be used to quell any tensions. The block guns fired out a 40mm wooden block that, when it hit a hard surface, would shatter into ragged pieces. When it struck a person, it left a terrible injury. If a solid block hit an ankle or wrist, it would break the bone. Removing pieces of wood was among the procedures I did, as well as removing cysts and lancing boils.

The most unusual procedure I would be asked to perform was the occasional removal of tattoos from the neck and/or hands of one of the guys preparing to be released back out into society. The request would first have to come from the inmate to his counsellor, who would then refer it to the Institutional Security &

Investigation Squad. Once they approved the request, it went to the chief medical officer to determine how it would be done and by which doctor. Removing tattoos from these particular places was an attempt to help the inmate being released to gain employment without any prejudicial discrimination against them.

The reason all requests had to go through the Institutional Security & Investigation Squad (commonly called 'Gooners') was to verify whether a particular tattoo was gang-related. They would determine if the person had a legitimate reason for it to be removed. The procedure to remove a tattoo was either by burning it off, or cutting it out and stitching the skin together. The chief medical officer would make the decision based on the size of the tattoo and location. For me, the most disturbing case came from a Jewish inmate who had, for some reason, chosen to be associated with the Aryan Brotherhood. To prove his loyalty, they had required him to put a swastika on one side of his neck and lightning bolts on the other, as well as a Nazi war eagle in the centre of his chest. I had seen this guy in the visiting room when his parents came to see him. His mother would always be holding his hand and sobbing. His father sat with his back to him while reading the Torah, and I had noticed that the collar on his coat was torn back.

I had the opportunity to speak to a Rabbi visiting

the prison. I mentioned what I had seen and asked if he could explain what it might mean. He said that by the style and colour of the clothes I had described the parents wearing, in all likelihood they were practising Orthodox and based upon what I believed to be their ages, he felt they may have also been survivors of the horrors of the Holocaust. It had been determined that the tattoos would have to be burned off to prevent any accidental cutting of a neck artery or vein. I asked him why he wanted them removed, and he explained that his mother had been trying to convince his father to allow him to parole home. Finally, after five years, his father agreed, but only if he had the neck tattoos removed. I asked, 'Aren't you Jewish, and if so, why would you be wearing Nazi symbolism?'

To which he responded, 'My parents are Jewish, but I am one hundred per cent Aryan.' I quizzed him on how that worked, and he said that I would never understand what he had to put up with listening to them speak about what they experienced in Poland as children. They would even show the tattoos that had been placed on their forearms when they were put in concentration camps. He, however, felt that having been raised in California, that he was 'really white' and American and being Jewish was dirty and foreign. After I did the procedures and watched him walking away, I kept thinking how terribly sad it was for someone to be so ashamed of their culture and history that they felt the need to try to hide it in such a hateful way. Although I only met him briefly, the memory has haunted me ever since.

The most disturbing thing I saw while working in the clinic was in the medical sergeant's office, where there was a whiteboard that kept tally of the number of inmates who had been beaten up, stabbed and killed, as well as those who committed suicide. It wouldn't have been so bad if its purpose was to keep records (though there were incident log books for that). This board was what the guards used to wager bets. I also overheard a couple of guards talking about how they could raise a tally, 'hedge their bets' by merely dropping a 'fake' chrono in the right area, which gave the appearance that the named individual on it was a 'snitch' or a 'paedophile'.

They would do this just to try to win the betting pool for the month, and I imagine they were not the only ones. Such was the life of an inmate at Folsom and, to my knowledge, I never heard of this at any other prisons in California.

For those who worked in the medical clinic, privileges included cooking our own food. We would cook for any patients and even some guards, who would patrol through. It was the same food that all inmates were served. The kitchen would send up the makings of each meal, and we had our own small kitchen equipped with a large fridge/freezer, stove and oven. The fact we were only feeding around 20 people meant we could season it to be more flavourful.

We also had access to showers with a degree of privacy. We could be by ourselves instead of having to bump shoulders, elbows, butts and any other body part with the guys on either side of you. The only drawback was the mature female staff nurses who would offer to come in and wash your back. Though I know some did take up the offer, I saw it for what it was. That is the opportunity to go to Ad Seg, and delay going home if caught. If people were caught, it always came out in the report that the inmate had pressured the nurse into 'engaging in acts of unwanted sexual nature' and the inmate would have charges of rape placed on them from Sacramento County district attorney, who had a 90-95 per cent success rate in winning a prosecution. For me, the risk was too great and the rewards marginal at best.

The best perk was access to a washer and dryer for cleaning our clothes. The policy at Folsom at this time was, you would be issued one complete set of new clothes when you arrived, and then you would receive a 'new issue' every year on the anniversary of your arrival. They would stamp your CDC prisoner number on your shirts, trousers, T-shirts and boxer shorts. If they found any clothing with a prisoner's number on it being thrown away and that prisoner was still there, a charge of 'misuse of state property' would be levied. The inmate would be required to pay three times the cost for replacement.

As, at that time, there were no laundry facilities provided by the prison, an inmate would hand wash everything issued to them including their bedsheets and towels, except the wool blankets which you could exchange every three months. The sinks in each cell were only about half the size of the average bathroom sink in a modern home. So, it is easy to understand how hard it was to wash clothes. You might be able to get a five-gallon bucket from someone in the kitchen, though these were never free – often they would cost $15 to purchase, or if you could find someone willing to rent out theirs, it would be a packet of cigarettes or $1 in canteen items. It was illegal to be in possession of a five-gallon bucket, mainly because so many guys used them to make 'pruno' – homemade prison wine. If found, the bucket would be confiscated and the inmate would get a write-up that would add anywhere from three to six months to their sentence.

If you lost a bucket someone had rented you, despite the fact it might have been confiscated during a cell-search, the backlash could be serious. Not only would the person it was confiscated from have to reimburse the bucket's owner (usually twice the cost, so $30), but they would also have to wash that man's clothes until he had a replacement bucket. On more than one occasion, a guy was stabbed over the loss of a bucket and refusal to do the other guy's washing. Inmates would clean out their toilets with a heavy-duty cleanser (Ajax was the most common) and then wash their clothes in the toilet, although the suction when flushed would sometimes snatch a sock or pair of boxers right out of your hand. You would always know this had happened on your tier by the sudden shout, 'Ah, son of a bitch, the toilet ate my sock'. The funniest I heard was, 'Damn, it took the whole sheet'. Though a single sock might not plug up a toilet, a bedsheet certainly would. If the plumbers had to be called out to clear the pipe, once the inmate was identified they would have to pay a fine for the plumber's time and the replacement of the sheet, and get months added to their sentence. What I always thought was wrong about this was that it would be the inmate plumbers who cleared the clog, and they only made about $18 a month, yet the fine was at the rate a free plumber might charge, so something like $25-$30 an hour. Working in the clinic allowed for a hustle of charging other inmates to take their clothes in and wash them in the machines at a rate of $3 a load – and it had no shortage of customers.

I started to make miniature motorcycles out of lolly

sticks (popsicle sticks in the US), as a way to cope with my situation. The canteen would sell hundreds of lollies every time it was open, especially in the summer when the daily temperature ran between 95 and 100 degrees on average. There was a guy I knew from Folsom, who had become a yard snipe, as he had no pay number and no money coming in from outside. He would do odd jobs to try and get a cigarette, and often he would be burnt by the guys not paying. As I didn't care for him being played for a fool, I hired him to get me lolly sticks and wash them, for which I would pay him a pouch of Bugler tobacco for every bundle of 50 sticks. That was 50 lolly sticks for a pouch of tobacco that cost me 80 cents, which meant I was paying 1.6 cents apiece for the sticks. On a good day, he might bring me 200-250. Of course, once he had a couple of pouches, I wouldn't see him again until he was out, but he knew I was always good to my word. That was the one thing I made sure of, even if someone didn't like me, everyone knew I was fair and my word was good. That was the one thing no one could take from me. The bikes I made with a little help from others to get the glue, sandpaper and paint, all of which I paid for, were about eight inches long. It would take about eight to ten hours to build from scratch once the lolly sticks were glued. I sold them for $10-20 dollars, depending on how detailed the work was.

Chapter 17

HAUNTED BY RETURN TO FOLSOM

When I returned to Folsom State Prison in 1999, it was a completely different place. It was no longer listed as a level 4 maximum security prison, instead it had been downgraded to a level 2, minimum/medium security prison. The average age was now approximately 32. The population was nearly double what it had been 15 years earlier. In most of the buildings on the yard, there had been federal court orders to make them single cell occupancy as they were too small to adequately accommodate two adult men. However, the court order had allowed for a clause which warned that if Folsom State Prison did not comply within six months of the order being issued, there would be a fine levied against them for every month it was in violation. You might think this would have encouraged Folsom to do as ordered. But all they did was write the fine into their annual budget – even though the court order had been issued 10 years earlier. The average cell size in all the buildings, except for #4 Building and #5 Building, were four feet wide by eight feet deep. These cells had an open bar front. I actually preferred a cell in #5 Building. Even though the walls were solid granite blocks, the door was made of solid steel with only a small viewing slot and approximately 30 holes 1¼ inches in diameter, which provided light from the tier and minimal ventilation. The upside was that as it was 6½ feet wide and eight feet deep, two people could easily move around. #4 Building had the same dimensions, but had open bar fronts and was used to house primarily mental health inmates.

The feeling at Folsom had really changed in the last 15 years. The first thing I noticed was all the 'heavy' fully active old gang guys were gone. They had been given indeterminate SHU terms and sent to Pelican Bay State Prison. The prison authorities hoped to resolve all the controlling gang problems, but all they really did was remove the only sense of order the prisons knew. So, in place of the AB and BGF, you had more guys from street gangs trying to take over. There was less politics but more aggression and violence, because these new groups were more interested in trying to make money by selling contraband drugs and cell phones. Fortunately for the rest of us, that meant that if you weren't trying to get in with them, you generally didn't get any grief from them. That is except the whites, who were now mainly controlled by skinheads, all under 30 years of age (the one exception I know of was a 70-year-old guy called 'Papa Skin'). They wanted to make money from drugs too, but would get all twisted up when a white Crip came onto the yard. These confrontations never ended well, as Crips stick together and tend to ride hard when pushed, often aided by other black inmates.

When I first returned, I was lucky enough to be housed in #5 Building, though unlucky to be placed in a cell with a guy named Chuck. There were a couple of issues. First, he did an in-cell hobby – although we had no choice, as the hobby shop was only for ordering and picking supplies. However, his hobby was stone work. He would often get stones from the yard, usually California Jade and Folsom Black Granite. Then he would sand the stones down in the cell. This would leave a fine dust on everything, including my bunk. Though he had been in the cell first, he had taken the upper bunk. Normally, I would have appreciated the bottom bunk. However, due to the dust, I did not like it, particularly when I found out that the dust from California Jade contained not only silica but also asbestos. Though he wore a face mask when he was working, never once did he tell me about the danger in the dust, so you can imagine when I found out, it caused a conflict I knew would only be remedied by one of us changing cells.

The other annoying thing, which not only bothered me but would get raised eyebrows from most guys on the yard, was that he would invite guards into the cell to show off his handiwork. He would make rings, keyrings, tie pins and pendants using the Folsom Black Granite that he would get sliced extremely thin by a guy who worked on the lower yard. He would then inlay the intertwined 'FSP' for Folsom State Prison into the stone using gold wire. He was not only quite talented, but very artistic. The two most amazing pieces I ever saw him make were, firstly, a bracelet of graduated hearts with a big centrepiece heart that opened up like a locket to hold a picture. He made the hinges and the clasp from gold wire. In the other piece, he replaced a face in a wristwatch using a piece of the granite and made the minute and hour hands with small cell keys on the tips. It took me four months to buy my own cell and move out, though I only made it four cells down the tier.

If you had your own cell and the right connections with inmates working in the maintenance shops, you could get it fixed up rather nicely. By the time I arrived back in Folsom, I had done enough time to know that my cell was my home, so I might as well make it as comfortable as possible. I had the small cell sink taken out and had installed a utility sink that was about 16 inches deep. You might wonder why I wanted such a large sink. Quite simply, there were times when we got locked down and didn't get to shower for a week or more. I was able to hang a curtain from my ceiling, and then I would be able to stand in my sink and shower in relative privacy. Having the option to wash my clothes in that large sink was nice. Folsom had started using the laundry bag system a couple of years after I left, which meant you put your dirty laundry into mesh bags to be sent to another institution to be washed and then returned a few days later, that is if the system worked properly, which it rarely did. You had one bag for your blue clothes and one bag for your whites, but under no circumstances were you allowed to send in your personal clothes to be washed by the state. There were guys who stupidly sent their personally-purchased blue jeans, or sweat track clothes, which would often get stolen.

I had also added a laminate countertop piece, which gave me roughly a foot and a half space on each side of the sink to use as a work table. The best improvement I made was to have the stainless-steel toilet removed and replaced with a nice porcelain one with a wooden seat. If you have never sat on a stainless-steel toilet in the winter, you cannot appreciate the changeover!

Strangely, the guards seemed to turn a blind eye to any improvements us old-timers made.

I had been back at Folsom for about a year when I was given a little snot-nosed kid, who had been pushed out of the California Youth Authority for intimidating female staff, to be my celly. Here was someone who was under 19 years old and had only been in an adult prison for less than a day, and the first words out of his mouth to me were, 'No disrespect, but I need to see your paperwork'. I was taken back, not even, 'Hello' or 'What's your name', just that he wants to see my paperwork. Without any hesitation, I dug through my property box, pulled out my classification sheet, which listed the charges I was in prison for and as he was starting to put sheets on his bunk, I tossed them to him. He said he would give me his papers, but I told him, 'You're too fucking young to be asking for my paperwork, so when you pull out yours, you better have your dad's as well.' I then left and went to see the housing clerk and said, 'I don't know whose idea it was as a joke to put that kid in my cell, but they better damn well get him out.' I knew the housing clerk quite well, and when he asked me what the problem was, I told him that the kid had asked me for my paperwork. He started to laugh. He assured me he would be moved by chow time, a couple of hours away, and I told him I'd pay him on canteen day. Back in the cell, the kid had read my paperwork and was handing it back while also presenting his. I told him I didn't care to see what he was in prison for, as his attitude told me all I needed to know. I advised him not to get comfortable as he would not be there for long.

About an hour later, the housing clerk came by, and told him to roll his stuff up as he was moving to #2 Building. The shock on his face gave me a certain amount of pleasure, as I was sure that the cell he was going to would not be as nice as mine, and he would probably find himself housed with someone who would not be as respectful as I would have been, had he come in with the right attitude. A couple of days later, I was approached by a couple of the young skinheads about the plight of my ex-celly. He had been placed on the fifth tier, on the back bar of #2 Building, with a guy nicknamed Stank. This guy was about six feet tall, and four feet wide who spat on the floor, had a tendency not to change his clothes or shower regularly, and was just an inconsiderate slob who made every celly miserable.

These guys had explained to my ex-celly that I was one of the last people he should have challenged for paperwork, and they were hoping that by speaking with me, I would allow him to give me an apology and move back in. I told them, very straightforwardly and emphatically, there was not a chance. This was a life lesson for him to learn to be a bit more respectful to those much older than he was. The kid only lasted about two weeks with Stank before they had a fight over a Snickers bar the kid had, which resulted in Stank going to Ad Seg and the kid going to the hospital before being transferred to another prison.

About this time, I met this surly guy with a British accent, though when I asked him about it, he rather rudely explained that although he may have been born in England, he was Irish, as were his parents. Trying to repair the damage, I greeted him in Gaelic, thinking that might be enough for us to at least have some conversation. That just seemed to upset him even more.

About three days later, he finally came back to see me and told me that though he was Irish, his parents didn't teach him any. Instead, they wanted him to be capable of growing up in England with as little stigma as possible. The fact I could speak some Irish, even though I was not fluent, had caught him off guard. He asked me how I had learned the language, and I told him it was through my mum (I had not yet discovered that she wasn't my mother, just the woman who had brought me from the Isle of Man), but as I had learned Gaelic as a child, I had a limited vocabulary. He started sharing about his family and life back in the UK. When he learned that I had been born on the Isle of Man and that would make me a British citizen, he asked if I was in contact with an organisation called 'Prisoners Abroad'. He suggested I write to them, as they supported British citizens in prisons all over the world, and he believed they might even be able to help me.

A few days later, he gave me their address and that very night I penned a letter to them. Little did I know then that this would be a pivotal point in my life, as they would get me the pen pal who became instrumental in helping to prove to the British authorities that I was a 'British citizen' and do the research that would allow me to learn about my family in the UK. I would also become their longest client, of 17 years, before I would step off a plane at Heathrow airport and head towards a whole new life – but that is another story.

Another interesting character I met in my second time at Folsom was called, 'Hound Dog'. He lived just down the tier from me and worked out in the recycling yard. Even then, the California prison system was way ahead of the rest of the world as they had a full crew of more than 40 inmates who would separate everything that came out of the prison in rubbish containers. However, when it was bins from the kitchen, you would be amazed at the number of guys who went to see if there was anything still edible in it. Hound Dog, being one of the lead men in the recycle yard, had the rights to first pickings, but he was known not to be greedy and always left a lot for his crew. Sometimes, in one of the bins from a building or the administration offices, there would be leftover food from a staff party. This is what Hound Dog called 'yummy trash'.

One of the best bins he ever searched was when the staff had a big going away party for a captain and the warden's secretary, on the same day. There was so much left over, especially cake, that Hound Dog was talking about it years later in great detail. There was always a laugh when he would get a new celly, usually some youngster, and he would make the guy a sandwich. The guy would always go out to the yard and brag about the great sandwich that Hound Dog had made him. Everyone who heard him would start laughing, and finally they would tell him he had just eaten a 'Yummy Trash Sandwich'. Funnily enough, I never heard of anyone getting ill from one of his sandwiches, but as I knew where he got the fixings from, anytime he offered me one I would politely say no and tell him I had just eaten, but to be sure and enjoy it anyway.

While at Folsom the second time around, I had jobs working in the hobby shop as the ordering clerk. The job was only a half-day assignment, but I was lucky enough to get paid for the whole day. I also worked in the clothing room (as they were both under the same supervisor) sorting out (almost) clean clothes that came back washed. One perk was that every week we would be given a new issue of clothes (two blue shirts, two blue jeans, four white T-shirts, four white boxer shorts and six pairs of socks), which we could either keep for ourselves or sell. A new set of clothes would fetch around $10, though you might get a bit more if you were willing to take some cosmetics as part payment.

The hobby shop was one of the more enjoyable jobs, even though at the time there was no actual shop. It should have been called the hobby office. As the ordering clerk, I was exposed to all the different things guys made, and I was often impressed. We had guys doing museum-quality plank-on-plank sailing ships, and the number of talented painters was staggering. One of the best would do aerial combat scenes from WWI right up to Vietnam, and many of his paintings made their way into museums and veteran's organisations. He sold some for as much as $5,000. Many guards who were veterans bought some of his smaller ones, for hundreds.

Inmates were allowed to purchase India ink for drawing purposes, as tattooing was a favourite pastime in prison, and you could get no better ink than India. The problem was, the prison staff knew that fact as well and so had limits on how much an inmate could buy.

Folsom prison was one of the favourite stopping points for tourist buses, and so there was a lot of business in the hobby craft store outside the front gate, right next to the Folsom Prison Museum. Every week, we would have anywhere from a few hundred dollars in sales up to even a couple of thousand dollars. Inmates would sell everything from a simple piece of Folsom Granite glued to a piece of cardboard called a 'Folsom Prison Weather Rock' for $2 each (they would sell 20-30 a week), to artwork, knitted items and wood crafted items. The two wood craft items that sold best and pulled in the higher prices were the 'working gallows' and the 'Beds with a girl on a box under it'. The latter was made exclusively by Cameron Hooker, a rapist, who had kidnapped a girl and kept her as a sex slave in a box under his and his wife's bed for years. He was one of a few sex offenders who had received protection from the AB. They didn't see what he had done wrong, as most of them liked the idea of having a sex slave themselves.

For eight months, while the hobby office was closed, I was re-assigned to China Hill. Folsom prison sits in a bit of a valley between two hills, as it had been carved out when the mining of the granite was done. China Hill is said to be where the Chinese workers were housed during the construction of the walls. We were on China Hill to grow vegetables that were transported to community programmes, like homeless shelters, senior centres, foodbanks and soup kitchens to help the poor in Sacramento. The other side was the hill where all the prison industry shops were – the licence plate factory (where all the metal plates for vehicles in California are stamped out), metal fabrication, paint shop and the all-important warehouse (from which all goods would be sent to other parts of the state). What you can't see any longer is the infamous, 'Bug House' that once briefly stood on the edge overlooking the American River.

The 'Bug House' had been built at Folsom to house mentally ill inmates and, like the prison itself, had been built from Folsom Black Granite. Though it had been completed, it was never officially opened.

Suddenly, it was all torn down, the granite was buried on site and for the most part forgotten. The uncon-firmed rumour that circulated around the prison is that four inmates had been placed in the building, only for it to be found the next day that three had died mys-teriously, and the fourth was in a catatonic state. And so things stood until January 16, 2001, when a parolee (reported as being disgruntled with Governor Grey Davis over being held at Patton State Hospital) drove his fully-loaded lorry into the State Capitol Building at 50 miles an hour, crashing it and killing himself. The Senate had been in session shortly before the crash, just above where the lorry came to rest in a massive fireball. The Capitol had been built with Academy Black Granite, which is no longer available, so a request went out for the prison to provide Folsom Black Granite instead. The granite was no longer being harvested there, so a decision was made to dig up the granite that had been used for the 'Bug House'.

One morning on the top of China Hill, where I worked in the greenhouse, I noticed inmates staring across to the other hill, where a big digger was busy. Not much gardening got done, as everyone, including the guards assigned to watch us, watched the stones being unearthed. The whole thing took three days until they had got the size and number of blocks of granite they needed to repair the Capitol. There were no longer any places west of the Mississippi River where the granite pieces could be cut and shaped, so all the stone was shipped to the east coast, brought back and installed. The differences between Folsom Black and Academy Black were indistinguishable to the average person, and the Capitol is now back to its former glory.

The best job I had by far was being the captain's clerk as it had even better perks, such as being allowed to work on my own legal work, access to a copy machine, and use of the refrigerator and microwave oven. When a lockdown did happen, I would be one of the first to come out of it, even if the whites had been the reason for it to begin. I was responsible for doing the Daily Activity Report (DAR), record and file all search logs, coordinate staff transportation teams, type up and distribute CDC 135s (inmate transfer orders between institutions), record, and file all rule changes from headquarters in Sacramento. When it was time for me to be transferred from Folsom, the captain offered to use his influence to stop it if I wanted him. I told him, 'No, I have been here for almost six years, I need a change.' He told me he was having me sent to the Lifer Unit at Deuel Vocational Institution (which would turn out to be my last prison).

It would be remiss of me if I left my memories of Folsom without mentioning the many ghosts reputed to dwell there. Throughout some of the older prisons, there are rumours and even reported sightings of things that cannot be explained. Folsom is believed to be the most haunted state prison in California (though it may have a rival with Alcatraz). If you think of the history of violence and tragedy that has permeated the place since it first opened, is it any surprise people might believe it is haunted? Some so-called 'paranormal experts' have said a big reason for that is because the prison sits in a quarried hole of granite, which is laden with crystals. There are those who say that crystals hold electrical charges so they create an electrical barrier to prevent the spirits of those who die at Folsom from going to their after-life, whatever it may be.

I don't know if any of this is true, I can only talk about what I read in the logs and reports written by the staff. As I was the captain's clerk, one of my duties was to prepare the Daily Activity Report (DAR) for the captain, who would then present it to the warden, who in turn would send it on to Sacramento. The DAR reported everything that went on in a 24-hour period, even such mundane things as rubbish bins not being lined up correctly, or a light left on at the end of the shift. Once the reports were submitted to the captain, he would sign it and a copy would go into a log book.

I remember my first 'Unusual Occurrence' notice from the guard staff who had been assigned to Tower 13. They reported hearing some low moaning and the sounds of chains rattling, but found no evidence of anyone else in the tower building apart from the three guards. I had only been working as the captain's clerk for a few weeks, and I thought someone was trying to put one over on me, especially when I saw it was from Tower 13. Even though I had heard some ghost stories from the old-time prisoners that I met in 1984, I don't automatically get all worked up over things I can't explain. While I cannot say I am a believer in things like ghosts, UFOs and Bigfoot, I am willing to keep an open mind to the fact that there are things we still don't know. However, I know from having done so much time that it is a constant source of entertainment with inmates and staff alike to try and make others look foolish. As this was to be an official report that would find its way to CDC Headquarters in Sacramento and it was my job to ensure its accuracy, I chose to speak to the captain about it. To my surprise, he listened and then said, 'Write it up as it was given to you'.

When I brought the DAR in for his signature, he surprised me again, by handing me some log books. He told me to read them when I had the time, but not to take them from the watch office. The three log books were from years in the 1940s, 1960s and 1980s, and he had placed paper tags on some pages I assumed he wanted me to read. Sure enough, those pages all had reports of strange incidents involving Tower 13. As I read through the entries, they all seemed to have a certain similarity with what I had put in my report, though there was some additional information. I realised that I had access to log books in the archives which went back to the early 1920s, as well as photos dating back to the turn of the 20th century. I then started looking through to see what else I could find. There were many other reports of unexplainable happenings. I really began to wonder how it was that so many people took this seriously enough to report it, and that higher staff would sign off the report before it was sent to Sacramento.

There is a book written by Dennis Hauck called *Haunted Places: The National Registry*, in which it mentions Folsom State Prison. It tells the story of a prison guard who was killed in a riot in 1927. Though I know of no accounts of inmates seeing him, I did find dozens of accounts from guards, who say that on foggy nights, he can be seen walking the catwalk above the front gate.

The 'laundryman' was a heavily reported apparition. He would be seen walking down the back tier and as he neared the end he would always stop to look back to the front of the tier before entering the same cell every time. What made him so well-known was that there had been reports of inmates who lived in that cell seeing him come through the wall, look at them for a few moments while trying to say something before just vanishing. What seemed to give validity to this story was the number of staff and inmates who had seen him. Inmates in that cell would always ask to be moved, even if it meant moving to Ad Seg, which was not something taken lightly by prison staff.

Staff often reported hearing voices, though it was said they were actually 'whispers' coming from where the old morgue had been as well as the 13 cells of the old

Death Row. These cells housed 93 inmates prior to their hangings, which were all carried out between 1895 and 1937. In an act of cruelty, after the man in the first cell was hanged, the men in the other cells would be moved one cell over, closer to the hangman's noose.

Hundreds of reports were from guard tower 13. It was a three-storey tall tower set a bit away from the cell blocks and was used for extreme punishment on those inmates who were uncooperative. On its first floor, there were dungeon-type cells (which haven't been used in more than 80 years). There are reports of inmates in the early 1900s who were put in water-soaked canvas and leather straitjackets and tied to the walls. As the jacket dried, it would often cut off circulation to the arms and hands, which would not only be painful, but in some cases caused the loss of a part of a limb. It was said to be a place where screams and wailing were common-place. There have been sightings of inmates in shackles shuffling along, though most commonly reported are the sounds of moaning, or the security doors to cells opening and closing – even though they were welded shut in the 1970s.

In 2004, while I was there, a Catholic priest was asked to carry out blessings at the prison in the hope of driving away some of the paranormal concerns.

BEHIND THE GRANITE WALLS

Chapter 18

FAMOUS NAMES BEHIND BARS

I arrived at the California Men's Colony in the spring of 1986, knowing little about it, except that it was known to have lots of programmes that lifers wanted to take in the hope of convincing the parole board to let them go. It was also well known that many famous – and even infamous – people were housed, or had been, there. It had four small housing yards, called 'Quads', which each consisted of two buildings bordering a small yard. If it wasn't for the double wire fences (12-14 feet tall), topped with razor wire and a gun tower in the corner of the yard, one might mistake CMC as some kind of college campus. It was often referred to as either 'the Colony at Bispo' or 'Home to the Stars'.

During my stay there – which lasted for almost seven years (1986-1993) – I would meet and talk to a number of these 'celebrities', though I cannot say we were ever friends. The most notable were those in the Manson Family – Charles 'Tex' Watson, Bruce Davis and Bobby Beausoleil. There was also Herbie Mullins, Christian Brando (actor Marlon Brando's son), Ike Turner (of Ike & Tina Turner), Jim Gordon (drummer of the group Derek and the Dominos) and Charles Keating Jr. (who was involved in the Savings and Loan scandal in the 1980s). Keating's biggest problem was that the people most hurt by his financial scam were the elderly. Many had put their life savings into investing with him. It seemed like a good number of white and black inmates at CMC were related to some of his victims. He actually hired the Surenos to protect him.

CMC was so different that it took time for me to adjust to the much more relaxed environment. From the moment I arrived in the Receiving & Releasing unit (R&R), I could tell things were different. The inmates who processed us asked if we wanted something to eat, and when we said yes, it wasn't just an old peanut butter and bread sandwich. They gave us a cardboard lunch box, which contained a sandwich roll, a can of ham spread, lettuce, tomato slices, and a slice of cheese, as well as mayo, mustard and relish packs. There were two pieces of fruit (apple and orange), a bag of crisps, two cookies and a half-pint carton of milk. I thought, what in the world is this? No other prison where I had been had given out such a thing. When the guard called us up to the counter to be given our property that we brought with us, they actually smiled and asked us to check that nothing had been damaged. Again, what weird sort of politeness was this?

I was put in 'A' Quad. The Quads were laid out to service different groups of inmates – 'A' Quad was for general population inmates, capable of work and school / vocational training. 'B' Quad was mainly for those who had physical medical problems. 'C' Quad also dealt with some inmates in a psych programme. Most were paranoid schizophrenics in remission who were on overflow from 'D' Quad, which is where they placed heavily-medicated psychiatric inmates and some psychiatric inmates who weren't responding to treatment.

When Christian Brando arrived at CMC, due to his notoriety and who he was related to, even though he wasn't on psychiatric medication, the administration decided to place him in 'D' Quad as they figured that nobody would recognise him.

Going through the turnstile on 'A' Quad and heading for where I had been housed, I was amazed to look out onto the grass yard and see people lying down on sheets, getting sun tans. But the most disturbing part was to see other guys rubbing lotion or baby oil on the backs of those lying down. I could tell that a few lying down were not only wearing feminine-type panties, but appeared to have breasts as well. I just shook my head and continued on to my housing unit, thinking, 'I'm certainly not in Kansas anymore.' When the guard pointed me to my cell, he told me that my celly was at work, but the bottom bunk was for me, so I just put my stuff there. He gave me the key to my cell, which, at first, I refused to take, thinking that it must be a set-up.

It was one of the porters nearby who told me, 'Welcome to Disneyland, you'll never do sweeter time.' Going up to my cell on the second tier, it turned out that we had a window that faced out to the yard. I put my property boxes on the floor as both bunks were made up. Although I had been told the bottom bunk was mine, the unspoken rule was that the incomer had to take the top, more awkward bunk. I felt it was only respectful to wait for my celly. I changed out of my blue shirt and white T-shirt that I had transported in and put on a tank-top and sunglasses and headed for the yard.

As I walked round the track, I took in all the activities. There were guys playing tennis, a few playing handball, while the little weight pile didn't seem to be segregated as guys of different races were working out together. But the thing that really caught my attention were three guys, who all had to be in their late 70s or early 80s, with golf clubs, chipping balls off the back wall of the vocation building. After watching for a few minutes, I realised they had a small nine-hole putting green to play on after they did their initial driving against the wall. I was just coming around the corner near the weight pile when I heard the slapping of feet of somebody running up behind me. I quickly turned around and shoved the guy by way of his left shoulder straight into the bushes that lined the outside of the housing units, to which he responded quickly as he was pulling himself out of the bushes, 'What the hell was that for?' I explained I had a problem with people running up on me. He said all he was doing was running on the track. The idea of people running on the track was not something I had experienced at other prisons. When he didn't get an apology, he just carried on running except, as he would come by me, he would slow down and walk past.

After about an hour, I suddenly noticed out of the corner of my eye a shadow of what appeared to be somebody crouching down and moving up on me. I swiftly turned around with my fists clenched, locked and loaded, ready to knock him down when the guy suddenly threw his hands up above his head and said, 'Hey brother, it's okay. I was just trying to see your tattoos on your back.' He then said, 'You must have just got in, where'd you come from?' to which I responded

DVI, which left him with a startled look. He almost whispered, 'Gladiator School? Holy shit!' He then continued by saying, 'Oh man, this place is nothing like that. Usually the only violence you'll see here is when a couple of queens are fighting over some guy.'

I then saw a guy running out of building one, straight across the yard, having to leap over some sun bathers while heading towards the sergeant's office. Another three or four guys jumped up from different parts of the yard and appeared to chase after him. I must have had a confused look on my face as the guy I had been talking to told me that the five guys were all known as 'Snitches'. He explained that the rule of the yard is that we could only be in possession of 30 canteen ducats (yard money). Each was worth $1 and if you were stopped by a guard and searched, and they found more than 30 ducats on you or in your cell, they would confiscate the extras and give them to the sergeant. These confiscated ducats were then used to pay the snitches. The first two snitches who could provide verified information about a rule violation, usually involving drugs, alcohol, tattooing or loan sharking, would get paid. Often when one guy could see what was going on, whoever could get there fast enough to hear what the first guy was reporting to the sergeant would be regarded as the second verification. Once the information was verified, which usually meant something had been found or someone placed in cuffs, the first reporting snitch would receive between $10-$20 depending on the seriousness of the violation and the second snitch would get between $5-$10. Even though I was not planning any illegal activity, I made a point of imprinting those five guys' faces in my memory.

What made CMC so desirable for many lifers was that it offered some of the greatest opportunities to be found suitable by the parole board. At CMC there was the opportunity to take more than nine different vocation courses. There were also nine different Prison Industries Authorities. A person could earn between 25 and 75 cents an hour. Additionally, you had an opportunity to take college courses, from Cuesta Community College, Chapman University and California State University at San Luis Obispo as well as multiple distance learning colleges. However, the thing that the parole board liked most was that CMC offered more than 30 therapy classes and, if you were a lifer, it was to your advantage to take as many as possible.

The first thing you were told on arriving at CMC was that no violence towards another inmate or staff would be tolerated, and if found guilty of violating this rule you would immediately be transferred back to a higher level institution and never allowed back to CMC. A special chrono would be placed in your confidential

C-file, which only the parole board would be able to review, and which would most likely prevent you from being released from prison for many years.

As I had previously been assigned to work in the medical departments, because of my training as a Navy Corpsman (medic), I assumed that is where I would end up, and so I made arrangements to meet with the head nurse who did the hiring to present my CV. All was going well until she asked me what I was in for, and I told her first degree murder. She sat back in her chair, looked me straight in the eyes, and said, 'You cannot work in our clinic, as we don't let anyone with a crime of moral turpitude work around patients'. Then she had a guard rush me out and back to the yard.

'Moral turpitude' was a phrase I had never heard applied to me. I went to the prison library to look it up, and this is the definition I found – 'an act or behaviour that gravely violates the sentiment or accepted standard of the community'. It seemed as though this description would cover everyone in prison and, to my mind, several politicians! When I found out about the inmates who did work in the medical clinic, almost all were in for sex crimes. That made me wonder about the head nurse, but I figured in the long run she did me a favour. If I had worked around those guys, we would have clashed, and all I wanted was to go home in 1996.

I had met a guy called Ted, who was hooked up with the Russian mafia (made up mostly of ex-KGB and ex-Russian military) out of Sacramento, on the weight pile a couple of days after getting to CMC, when he asked me to spot for him. That meant assisting them in putting the weight bar back on the rack after your exercise. You had to work with somebody you could trust not to harm you. It turned out that he knew of me well before I knew of him. Ted worked in the PIA Shoe Factory and said he could get me a job there, which would mean we would be on the same work schedule and it wouldn't mess with our working out on the weight pile. I got assigned as a sole layer, something I had never done, but I picked up really quickly. Funnily enough, I would find out in 2009 that my great grandfather, George Kane, was a shoe and boot maker, running his own shop in Liverpool. I went from making 25 cents an hour to 40 cents in just two months, instead of the usual 90 days.

The job was all right. We were making the boots used throughout the California Department of Corrections, state work camps and some county jails. We produced 3,000-4,000 pairs of boots every week, ranging from a women's five up to a men's 22. Then came the order for 24 pairs of camp boots, sizes 18 to 22, all extra wide. The rumour went around that some professional or college basketball team must have been sent to prison.

The boot order that really raised everyone's curiosity was a thousand pairs in sizes $7\frac{1}{2}$ to 8, and we had to do it after the two regular shifts were done for the day. This meant working overnight with overtime pay, which people would jump at since the wages were so low. We were given just a week to get them packed up and shipped out. Only about a dozen of us were chosen and everyone was very efficient, giving the guy who was tasked with quality control and packing little reason to complain. We made the deadline and the next day the boss came in and handed out sodas to everyone who had worked on the project.

About a month later, we had some Federal agents come into the prison who interviewed inmate workers in the shoe factory, asking about a 'special' shipment of boots. I will give credit to the guys who had worked with me to get them done and dusted, as no one said a thing, just that we make boots every day and don't know where they go once we are done with them. Later, I found out from one of the shipping clerks that the boots had been meant to be sent to the Guatemalan Army, via a California Youth Authority requisition number. The US State Department wasn't involved. That is, until the Guatemalan government complained that they didn't get them, and there didn't seem to be a paper trail. I always thought they had been heisted from the warehouse, but perhaps a corrupt middleman along the way squirrelled them away.

CMC was a unique place, as the staff didn't like it being called a 'prison', they wanted things to be laid back and run smoothly, which is why they had stringent rules in regard to violence, bullying or even overt signs of disrespect towards staff and other inmates.

The full impact of the rule of no violence came about 18 months after I arrived. We had an older guy working in the glue pits of the shoe factory and one day he came to work with a black eye, though to his credit he tried to hide it by getting some concealer from a queen. But with the heat he worked around, the make-up ran, and he was found out. His supervisor called the PIA sergeant and made a report. It turned out three white gang dropouts wanted him to smuggle out some glue so they could sell it to people to use to get high. He had refused, so they punched him, and went to his cell and robbed him of everything of value. They told him they would be back that evening to get the glue or give him a real beating. He was so scared that you could see him shaking while recounting the story. When the guy went back to his cell, the aggressors were there for the glue. What they didn't know was that in the cell across and the ones on both sides, guards were posted up to listen and as soon as the guys made threats to the old guy, the guards came out and grabbed the three surprised inmates.

A few days later, the one who had been the leader of the three was transferred out of CMC and back up to Folsom, the place he had moved from after telling on the AB. He was heard screaming that he would be killed, and struggled with the guards who were placing him in the transport van. Less than a week later, word filtered down from Folsom that the first day he had been released to the yard he was stabbed multiple times and died from his injuries. Staff wanted those kinds of incidents to be widely known so those that wanted to be tough guys would re-think their decision.

The only real violence tended to happen when two queens fought over a guy. This could turn very vicious as not only would they pull hair and slap, but often swing fists and, in the most severe cases, even slash at each other with razor blades. However, when one of those incidents led to someone being cut, a queen got transferred out, and it was always to Atascadero State Hospital for the criminally insane.

People get the idea that queens are all soft and feminine. I have seen some extremely 'buffed up' queens on the weight pile, and more than a few had boxed before changing over to being a girl.

No matter what inmates might personally feel about

having queens on the yard, one thing that always brought everyone out to watch was when they played sports against the men's teams from the other quads, or especially when they played against a visiting team from a local college. Suddenly all the seats on the bleachers would fill up and there was hardly any place around the yard that someone wasn't standing. Out would come the 'Powderpuff' team, wearing short cut-off jeans, tied up tops, make-up, usually very bright red lipstick, swishing everywhere they went. Most of them were far from what anyone might say was attractive, and a few were even quite muscular. However, when it came to playing sports, especially baseball / softball, the Powderpuff team rarely lost and if the outside teams which played at a collegiate level were beaten by a group of convict queens, it took a toll on their feelings of manhood.

CMC was where I met and spoke to the more infamous inmates during my time inside. I met Charles 'Tex' Watson (who had been the right-hand man to Charlie Manson), who was the inmate pastor in the Protestant Chapel. He still gave off the air of charisma that allowed him to draw young girls to the Manson Family. Though, at this stage and place in his life, it was mostly young men he attracted who wanted to revel in his presence. I wasn't any more impressed with him than I had been with Charlie Manson, who I had met and had dealings with at CMF – Vacaville (I write about that in *34 Years in Hell*). 'Tex' and I had more than a few interactions over the seven years I was at CMC, because he lived right above me for nearly half that time. In building one, the third tier was designated the Honour Unit, and he had been housed there since the late 1970s. It was called the Honour Unit because inmates were allowed special privileges that the general population didn't get, such as not being locked in their cells apart from the hours of 2am-5am, being able to take showers whenever and as often as they wanted, and, most important of all, they were single celled. They were always the first to be allowed to go to the canteen and the gym, either when films were being shown or a special event was happening like a music show or outside speakers. This ensured they got the best seats and often got to meet people from the outside (almost like having a backstage pass).

Some of the least-liked guys I met at CMC were known as the 'Chowchilla Kidnappers', and consisted of two brothers – James and Rick Schoenfeld (who were at CMC when I arrived in 1986) – and Fred Woods (who arrived a year or so before I was transferred out in 1993). These three guys had been in their early 20s and each came from quite prominent families, when, in 1976, they hatched a plan to kidnap children to get millions as they were impatient for inheritances. They decided to take a school bus carrying 26 children aged 5-14 years old with only a 54-year-old bus driver named Frank 'Ed' Ray to watch over them, in Chowchilla, California. Luckily, none of the children or Mr Ray were seriously hurt, even though they had been transferred into a van that had been buried at a quarry owned by Fred Woods's family.

They were all initially sentenced to mandatory life sentences, but on an appeal were able to get their sentences reduced to life with possibility of parole. That led to years of support and pleadings by their family and friends. Younger brother Richard Schoenfeld was paroled in 2012 and James in 2015. It had always been presented that Frederick Woods was the leader and main instigator of the crime by the police investigators.

I once told the Schoenfeld brothers that they had been extremely lucky it was the authorities who had caught them. When they asked what I meant, I explained that one of the children on the bus had been related to a high-ranking member of the San Jose Chapter of the Hells Angels. As soon as word got out the bus was missing, the message spread through the motorcycle shops and clubs in the San Joaquin Valley to find the missing bus. There had been a bounty for finding the kidnappers, not to turn them in to the police, but rather to turn them over to the Angels. James' face went completely pale, and you could see that both of them were processing what I told them and realising I was right.

I knew Fred Woods had not yet been paroled, though I only saw him a couple of times, but I didn't know what was keeping him in prison. That is until recently, when I read that he had been running businesses from inside prison without notifying the prison authorities. In October 2019, he attended his 19th parole hearing, only to be denied. Now with declining health, he may not make it to his next parole hearing scheduled for 2024, and it is unlikely he will ever get the opportunity to enjoy the benefits of his business wealth.

Unique at CMC, on 'A' Quad was a bench just for lifers that was shaded by the 'Tennis Shoe Tree'. This tree got its name for having the tennis shoes of all the lifers from 'A' Quad thrown up into its branches as they paroled out of prison. I remember the first time I saw it; there must have been 50 pairs of shoes hanging from it. It was a strange but, in some ways, comforting sight to see as it meant guys did go home from CMC. I got to watch more than a few lifers go through the ritual.

After working in the shoe factory for almost 3½ years, I was offered the opportunity to work in the Prison Industries Authority – in laundry on the graveyard shift. It might not seem like a good job change, but believe me, it was, and the graveyard shift was the most sought-after one there. Work days were from 8pm to 6am on Sunday to Thursday. This allowed us to receive an extra day's pay for any holiday that fell on a Monday. The morning shift ran from 7am-2pm, so on a Thursday if the shift was short-handed, which it often was, we could go to breakfast and then come back and work another seven-hour shift. The supervisors always liked that, as we had a reputation for being the hardest workers in the laundry, and it was a win for us as we got extra pay.

The laundry jobs started at 20 cents an hour and could go all the way up to 75 cents by learning skills and supervisors putting you in for raises. The graveyard shift was so valued because everyone started at 30 cents an hour, but I had been making 55 cents an hour in the shoe factory, and so that is what I started on in the laundry. Less than a year late, I was making the top scale of pay of 75 cents, as I learned how to run the washers, dryer, sheet folding machines, ironing press decks, and coordinate the unloading and sorting of clothing off the truck. Often, I would be tasked with driving the 'mule', a motorised cart with two small trailers attached that went to the different quads and picked up dirty clothes.

Even in the laundry, there were hustles which guys could make extra money from. Staff generally turned a blind eye as it kept the peace. We did not just clean clothes for CMC. We had contracts to do the laundry for two state mental facilities – Atascadero State Hospital (one of the places where people with criminal convictions were kept) and Camarillo State Hospital (primarily civil commitments by the courts or families), as well as for the San Luis Obispo County Jail (inmates there burned down the jail laundry) and, finally, the California National Guard base down the road.

As the people in Camarillo State Hospital were not prisoners, only civil commitments, they were allowed to wear their own clothes, which they would often soil with urine and faeces. When the hospital staff took the dirty clothes off them, they rarely went through the pockets. When the clothes came to us in the laundry, the guys working the 'soil line' would go through the pockets – finding money, watches, jewellery and sometimes portable video games (which, sadly, many kept for themselves or to sell). On one occasion, wrapped in a sheet, a man's military medals were found and turned in to the laundry staff. It took a while to find out who owned them, and before they were returned to the hospital, one of our inmate workers made a shadow box in hobby class for them to be displayed in. The veteran's family sent a letter to the PIA laundry, thanking everyone for finding them and the gesture of helping to preserve them.

Two other things that would often be stolen from

the Camarillo laundry by inmate workers to try and make money from were hoodies (as we were no longer allowed to order them – the ones we had were under what the administration called the 'Grandfather Clause', meaning we could keep ours until they wore out), and women's panties, for which the queens would pay a good price. I always thought it was strange that families would buy for the women in a mental facility often quite expensive and 'sexy' undergarments. The penalty for being caught stealing the women's items was immediate dismissal from the job as well as a disciplinary write-up which would extend your sentence. However, as they were worth anywhere from $10 to $20 each, you can see why someone would take the chance.

There was a guy called Squirrel who worked in the laundry doing odd jobs, mostly cleaning up, as he seemed simple-minded to most who met him. A number of inmates played tricks on him, or tried to make him look foolish, as he never got mad and just seemed to take it in his stride, probably because it had been that way all his life. Whenever they had an opportunity, some guys would sneak up on him and, using a paperclip, hang a pair of panties off the back of his trousers so he would walk around and others would get a laugh. Sometimes someone would tell him and he would remove it with a laugh, but even the guards would find it funny and not say anything. It got to the point that when we would be getting 'patted down' on the way out in the mornings and Squirrel had a pair of panties hanging off him, the guard wouldn't say anything, just letting him go.

It was probably after three or four months of him taking out a pair several times a week that someone saw him hanging them on himself and then heading for the pat down. When he was caught, the supervisors didn't fire him because even though he admitted to it, they believed he had been put up by others as they did not think it was something he could plan. I think he was more on the ball than he was given credit for!

CMC had more openly gay and lesbian guards than anywhere else. This worked well for the queens and even the gay boys, and helped get a chapter of the Metropolitan Community Church established in the prison. This church, though a Protestant affiliation, has a special outreach to the gay, lesbian, bisexual and transgender communities and is said to have more than 200 congregations in 30 countries. At CMC, on every October 31, there would be a special Founder's Day celebration in the visiting room. That is where they had to hold their services as the Protestant chaplain would not allow them to set foot into the prison chapel, even though he would allow other denominations. At the Founder's Day celebration in 1992, one of the staff sponsors for the church, who was also the job steward for the guards at CMC, attended wearing a nun's habit, which upset some upper prison management. Though it may have been his Bert Reynolds-style moustache!

One thing that happened at all prisons, though it is often kept quiet, is inmate-staff sexual interactions. In very rare cases do these ever work out. Usually the staff member gets fired, or if it can be proven that they were bringing in contraband, they will find themselves in prison. The inmate is given a disciplinary for sexual misconduct at best, though some have been charged with rape and given an additional prison sentence. I saw no benefit to even entertaining the idea if it meant I would spend the rest of my life in prison.

There were a few cases that caused shockwaves. The first involved inmates and the music teacher. CMC was unique in that it had a fully equipped and staffed band room. There was a full-time music teacher with six inmates who were all trained musicians working for her. Any inmate who wanted to learn to play an instrument from guitar, drums, or horns right up to piano or keyboard could go for lessons and use the equipment, which was always kept in top-tuned shape. As the inmate workers were skilled and hard to replace, they were exempt from not only having to take other jobs, but were also pulled off buses when up for transfer.

Of course, when the teacher had worked for years with the inmates under her supervision, there is an opportunity for the blurring of the lines. At some point, she had become involved with one guy. It may have started innocently enough, but it crossed over into a sexual relationship. Every day, inmates not assigned to either the vocational shops or in one of the prison industry shops all had to report back to their housing units to be counted. This would take from 45 minutes to an hour to complete. There was, however, a loophole as staff members could elect to 'out count' an inmate under their supervision, by merely calling the watch office where inmate counts were recorded and saying they needed the inmate to stay at their assignment.

This is what the music teacher would do. At first, it may have only been once or twice a month, and it became once a week and finally almost every day during the working week. It had happened in such a way that other staff members didn't suspect anything and just started to out count the inmate automatically. It was about two years before another inmate worker caught on, and decided he wanted in on the action. The two inmates had been a part of the same gang at one point and had a certain loyalty to each other, and so now the music teacher had another who knew about the liaison. Whether out of her choosing or because she felt she had to protect her job, she started to have sex with both inmates. Of course, the more people who know you are up to something, the sooner it is likely to be leaked further, which is exactly what happened only six months after this new arrangement started.

When the Security & Investigation Unit (S&I) gets word of something, they will ride up without warning, bringing the full strength of their unit. At CMC, it was rare that there was much for them to do except to intercept a small amount of drugs, nothing like the other prisons where the S&I units were having to deal with large shipments of drugs, gang activity (inside and out of prison), stabbings, extortion, weapons and rapes. On rare occasions, this would involve staff misconduct. As little to none of the above seemed to happen at CMC, when something did happen, nobody wanted to be left out. This could be a moment of glory, as all participants in the raid would have their name on the report that went to Sacramento. So they had the full 'baker's dozen' of one lieutenant, two sergeants and 10 officers.

Everyone knew something was wrong, and soon there was an announcement that all housing units were to remain locked down until further notice. All inmate workers in the vocational shops and PIA shops had to return to their yards to lock up. Everyone who had a yard-facing window looked out to see what might be occurring, and shouted to the cell across from them with any possible news. Most feared a mass prison-wide shakedown by the guards. Speculation started to rise, with people calling out asking, 'Was there a stabbing?' 'Did they find a large quantity of drugs?' 'Did someone commit suicide?' or 'Was a staff member attacked?'

As the tier guard walked past on his rounds, you could hear the same questions being asked of him. The only response he gave was, 'I know as much as you guys do, or likely less, as I go home at night'. The lockdown lasted until the evening meal and even then, we were sent to the chow halls in smaller groups, given five minutes to eat and then quickly ushered back to our cells without any explanation, even by the staff who were usually pretty friendly. This told me it was something quite serious, yet they had not done a shakedown, so whatever happened must have been on a different yard or involved only inmates from a different yard. I felt sorry for the last group of guys to go to chow as it was about three hours after normal feeding time. Just like any other zoo, the animals get used to eating at a certain time and change tends to make the animals grumpy.

This was the way it was for two days, escorted to chow and straight back to the cell, except I worked in the PIA laundry on the first watch shift. When the laundry for the outside paying customers was needed, all of us on that shift were escorted to work. As our crew comprised inmates from the three mainline yards, we were able to compare notes and quickly ascertain that the incident involved guys who lived on 'C' Quad. Other guys said that two guys who had worked in the band room had not returned to their cells, and then the Gooner Squad had snaffled up another three who worked there.

Finally, on the third day, the whole prison came off lockdown and everyone headed off to their assignments such as, education, kitchen, vocation shops, etc. By the end of the day, the whole story had been pieced together about the music teacher and the two inmate workers' sexual escapades. Of course, now the speculation began, if it was consensual, or a forced activity. It seems that when the S&I Unit had carried out their midday raid, they found the music teacher in a compromising position with the two inmates, and all three were in stages of being undressed. When this information got out, all at CMC knew it would be extremely costly for those involved, with the inmates likely to face new charges that would add years to their sentences.

When the investigation was finished and the report filed, the full story was able to get out to the inmate population. The music teacher was found not guilty of bringing in any contraband, but guilty of entering into a consensual sexual affair with the first inmate (she had been married). She was fired, losing any pension, and could never get another teaching or state job. In essence, her career and livelihood were over.

The two inmates didn't fare well either. The first inmate was found guilty of being 'involved with a consensual sexual act with a state worker', but received only a disciplinary write-up. But the prison authorities took away one year's worth of earned good time. Because he was a lifer, that write-up would cost him at least 10 years in denials from any parole board. The second inmate, who was actually found to have coerced the music teacher into performing sexual acts by threatening to tell on the pair, was found guilty of 'receiving sexual favours by threat or force'. His actions were referred to the San Luis Obispo County district attorney office, who filed rape and other sexual offences against him. He was found guilty of all charges and was given another 20 years on top of his sentence.

The other big scandal at CMC was when it was discovered that the warden's secretary had been having sexual encounters for nearly four years in the administration office with an inmate. This only came out after she had retired from her job at CMC and was receiving her pension. She had applied to not only come visit the inmate who had been one of the porters, but additionally she had filed a petition to marry him. To say that this was a shock is a huge understatement, as she had worked for six wardens over her 25 years in service, and no one had any idea this was going on. The warden who had been in post when she retired had been her boss for seven years, and he couldn't believe she had been able to pull this off without him noticing something amiss.

He immediately had the inmate taken roughly from his cell and straight to Ad Seg, where he remained for the best part of three months, while the ex-secretary had to speak to investigators, and even eventually hire herself an attorney to protect her and her fiancé's rights. It may sound over the top, but the warden felt that he had been the victim here, and that they had intentionally done this to him to try to ruin his reputation. When it had all been thoroughly investigated and nothing came to light apart from possibly some lightly veiled flirting, the inmate was released from Ad Seg. The attorney had even got a 'cease and desist' order from the local court to prevent the warden from transferring the inmate, who only had a couple of years left. The visiting application form was approved and the marriage petition granted. They got married at the prison about six months after she had left. I wonder how the warden felt having to approve their request for conjugal visits in one of the prison's family visiting apartments.

In a similar scandal, my counsellor on 'A' Quad was involved in a sexual affair with her clerk in the office and, again, this was one of those affairs that happened during the lunch lockdown count time. It would only happen when all the other counsellors were out of the office for either lunch or meetings. This affair, like the warden's secretary, had been going on for years and when all the facts came out, it was revealed that the counsellor had been over to the inmate clerk's family home for meals and had actually gone on holidays with his family. However, once again, S&I got wind of their tryst and proceeded with an investigation, which then led to yet another raid, which found them engaging in illegal sexual behaviour. This one did not have a good outcome. She had been a counsellor II (the supervisor over the other counsellors), and she had sensitive and classified information in her office, which she had allowed her clerk to help review and file away. That act alone would have been enough to get her sacked, but the fact they were carrying on a sexual relationship added fuel to the fire. The issue that brought up charges and got her sent to prison was the fact that when they went to the inmate's cell, they found not only naked photos she had given him and photos taken when she was on holidays with his family, but she had actually provided him with contraband items, such as a CD player, cans of food, ink for tattooing and a gold ring with a diamond in it. Collaborating evidence had come from letters she had sent to him, using a false name and a P.O. Box with a return address, which they were able to trace to her.

The inmate was a lifer and more than 30 years later, he was still in prison having to try to explain this liaison to every parole board panel he appeared before. The ex-counsellor was found guilty of a number of violations, and the state made an example of her. She was given a sentence of more than 20 years, and you have to wonder if she felt it was worth it? Did she stay with the guy and receive support from his family while she was doing time?

CMC was so completely different from every other prison I experienced. Most of the prisons allowed inmates to wear some personal clothing. In most cases, only items like blue denim jeans were approved (though no stonewashed or fancy designer ones). You could have grey or white T-shirts, but only blue chambray-type outer shirts. We were allowed white or grey sweat / tracksuits (though it had to be either light grey or heather grey only). Tennis shoes were allowed with the exception of Calvin Klein and British Knights brands. Crip gang members wanted to wear the BKs to make a statement that they were 'Blood Killers' and the Bloods wanted to have CKs to convey the fact they were 'Crip Killers'. Even though it may be a white or Latino who tried to order them, they would still be denied on the grounds that they could cause an issue with safety and security if a fight broke out over the shoes. Generally, inmates were not allowed to possess clothing or shoes that had any shade of red, green, brown or black.

At CMC, it was different. Other than the rule about wearing only blue jeans, although they did allow stone-washed jeans, and the restriction on no red, brown or green clothing (brown or green are the colours of the guard's uniform), every other colour was fine. But I nearly fell foul of the rules. I had been working out and attained a 54-inch chest and nearly 19 inch biceps, and found that most standard shirts were a tight fit. I had found in one of the approved vendor catalogues that there were what were called 'Buccaneer Shirts', that had a bit of extra room in the chest, shoulders and arms. There was a special discount of three for the price of two. I chose one white, one black and just for a change, one purple top. I figured there would be no problem as I had stayed away from the prohibited colours.

I had to go to the package room when they arrived, where a guard checked each order to ensure that no contraband was coming in. As he started to hand me my shirts, he stopped and held up a shirt that certainly wasn't purple, but appeared to be more of a tone of red. The guard said, 'You know you can't have red shirts.' I said I had ordered a purple one. Unlike most guards, he actually pulled out the invoice. He said they had run out of stock on purple, so had sent the closest they had, which was listed as Oxblood. Taking another quick look at the shirt and the invoice, he suddenly handed me the shirt while remarking that 'It really did look like it was red, but I guess that is my mistake, as it is actually Oxblood, which isn't on the restricted list'.

I quickly signed the receipt card, which would prove that the shirts had been issued to me by a staff member. I expected that I would not be keeping the 'Oxblood' shirt long, but I was going to enjoy it. I went to find the inmate cameraman as I wanted to get a photo in it just to be able to prove this actually happened. As soon as the photo was arranged, I quickly changed into my 'Oxblood' shirt, then hit the yard and got the photo done. It was my celly, Jim, who after we had gone through the initial banter of what colour it was, said, 'Wait a minute it is red, that's not Oxblood, it is OX BLOOD, like the colour of the blood from an Ox'. Somehow, the system had actually legitimately issued me a red shirt.

As I figured, I only had it for about two weeks when a sergeant saw me wearing it and pulled me up. He asked how I got the shirt, and I told him it had been issued to me by staff in R&R. He didn't believe me and had me go get my receipt to prove it, which I happily did. He studied the form, then walked me to the watch office. He contacted R&R, and the particular guard was not only on, but admitted he had given me the items and didn't understand why there was a problem. The sergeant told him to come to the watch office.

The guard brought the R&R Lieutenant (his immediate supervisor) with him, and now there were about a dozen staff looking at my shirt, which the sergeant had me take off. I was amazed there were so many different opinions on what colour it was – burgundy, a reddish-purple, magenta, dark orange to even one saying it looked rose. Only the sergeant who had stopped me used the word 'red'. Then one of the inmate clerks got a dictionary. He read out the definition of Oxblood – 'It is the colour of deep red, with more of a hue of purple or dark brown'. You might think that would clear up any confusion, but it did not!

Out of his office came the watch captain, who had been listening for more than 20 minutes to the conversation. He took the shirt and made a decision, something the others had been unable to do. Looking at me, he said, 'Seeing this was not a mess of your making, the shirt will be confiscated and destroyed. You, however, will not get a write-up and the institution will refund you the money for your whole order. You can keep the other two shirts. I feel that is fair, what do you think?' I did not hesitate to agree, and then he told everyone to get out. I walked away with two shirts and $40 better off. That is what happens when you hire staff who are not required to have graduated from high school!

Like most things in prison, if you have some small privilege that makes you feel more like a 'real' person and not just a prisoner, someone will figure out a way to screw it off and that is exactly what happened over wearing personal shirts. A guy figured out how to escape from CMC by just walking out of the visiting room. The guy had convinced his girlfriend to visit with an extra set of clothes and some make-up. He had been planning this caper for well over a month, as he had shaved off all his facial hair and would go out to ensure his face was tanned. The night before the visit, he had one of the queens thin his eyebrows and teach him how to apply basic make-up.

The next day, his girlfriend arrived looking like she may be in the family way and so the guards didn't even pat her down. All visitors had access to toilets on the other side of the guard's podium. However, there were no barriers to prevent an inmate from going into one, except the keen eagle-eye of the guard on duty. His girlfriend went in and got rid of the excess clothing, a blond wig she had worn (it matched her hair colour). All visitors are given a stamp on their right hand that will only show up under fluorescent light, so they can verify who is a visitor and who is not. There was a locker near the entrance door where visitors place anything they can't bring in (purses, car keys, wallets, etc). The guy had his girlfriend lick the area where the guard had placed her stamp, and then rolled her hand over the back of his right hand to transfer a portion of the stamp. When the moment was right, he gave a signal to another guy in visiting to start a screaming match with his partner, thus distracting the guards. With this being a Sunday, there were far too many inmates in the visiting room and the guards were short-staffed.

He snuck into the ladies toilet, quickly changed into the women's clothing from the wig right down to some rolled-up slippers, did a bit of make-up and was ready to leave. He went to the lockers and retrieved a small purse and a set of car keys, then headed for the visitors' exit. As there had been a change of guards on the outside door, all they did was scan his hand with a UV light to ensure that there was a stamp and wave him through, being none the wiser. The guy quickly headed to his girlfriend's car and drove out of the prison. A few miles away, he pulled into a gas station, went in and changed into some men's clothing she left in the car. Then he called to have a taxi pick up his girlfriend from the prison. When it arrived at CMC, the outside guard called to let her know and, after checking the stamp on her hand, she was off to meet up with her guy.

They drove straight down to Mexico and across the border, and it was about six months before they were located and brought back to California. He got a year added to his sentence, she got two years for helping him to escape, and all the rest of us were told we could no longer wear our personal 'men's' shirts to visiting. Many of us argued that he didn't leave in men's clothing. However, to try to save face, the prison administration took a hard stance, and we lost out.

CMC had a fantastic hobby programme and often did sales of more than $5,000 a month in the craft shop. In the height of the summer holiday season, it would even top $10,000. This was in part due to the fact that the town of San Luis Obispo was very popular with visitors and just a short distance from the prison, so they had the craft store open to the public. There were a number of artsy-type shops in the town centre and near the beaches. People would often come out to the prison and buy inmate craft work to sell in their shops, and some shop owners even had a contract with certain inmates to make custom items just for them. The inmates who found their work being resold in these fancy shops were those who made jewellery, ceramics and paintings. One guy made custom inlaid belt buckles and brooches, none of which sold for less than $100-$200. Some of his buckles fetched more than $500 in the shops. We could sell to prison staff as long as they had gone to the hobby manager and filled out the proper paperwork. Guards would often contract with the buckle guy. There was an Asian guy who would make designer wedding ring sets for a jeweller in town. His rings were never under $1,000 per set. Depending on the design, materials and stones, some even went for well over $5,000.

Most CMC inmates had a lot of money available to them, as we had nine PIA shops and the hobby craft shop. This gave an opportunity for an investment firm – Blakeslee & Blakeslee – to start giving classes in financial investment and planning. Inmates were able to invest through the firm into stocks, bonds and mutual funds, building up portfolios that, for a few risk-takers, would give them a financial worth of more than a million dollars. That eventually enraged victims' rights groups, who campaigned and had it stopped. The pendulum swung the other way, and there came a time in the mid-1990s when inmates weren't even allowed to have outside bank accounts.

In 1992, we got a new warden and deputy chief

warden, who decided that having trees on the yards was a security issue. They even went so far as to claim the inmates might jump out of the trees and attack the guards. One day, all the yards were locked down and all the trees and bushes were cut down. Even the lifer bench was removed. A few months later, many of the programming lifers, including myself, were notified that we were to be transferred, so the prison administration could change the make-up of the population. Most of us knew this meant the end to what CMC had been for nearly 20 years − a peaceful, programming prison where getting out was more important than being stupid and staying in.

The medical care at CMC was quite a bit better than it had been at my previous prisons of Folsom, San Quentin and Deuel Vocational Institution. They did a reasonably good job of replacing the lunate bone in my wrist (from when I had broken my hand at DVI before I transferred), except for the rather large scar on the back of my left hand. They gave me a lot of Darvocet and Percocet tablets for pain after the wrist surgery and, had I been of the mind to, I could have sold them on without any problem. I chose to flush them away, as I don't like taking any medication, and had never done illegal drugs. The only addiction I had ever had was to my motorcycles.

My cellmate, Jim, had a stunted right arm as a result of being a 'Thalidomide baby' and only had three fingers on his right hand, yet he would still try to work out on the weight pile. I had made him a set of custom leather gloves to help him get a better grip when lifting dumbbells. One day, he had been working on an incline bench with 40lb dumbbells. While he was trying to use his left hand to loosen the strap on his special glove on his right hand, Jim was sitting upright on the bench and had the weight against his chest. But the moment the glove strap came undone, the 40lb weight slipped and fell onto his crotch. There was a sudden and painful scream and a number of guys ran over to find out what happened. Apparently, the weight had landed on one of his testicles and after being taken to the clinic, it was discovered that he had a crushed testicle. Initially all they did was to give him a prescription to come to the clinic three times a day and get a bag of ice to help the swelling go down, and they gave him Motrin for the 'discomfort' he was feeling. 'Discomfort', what they hell were they talking about? He was in severe pain, so much so that other guys brought him some prescription painkillers they had been given.

It took me almost two weeks filing 602 Appeal forms for him to get assessed and treated. Finally, when he was seen by a doctor at CMC, he was sent out to French Hospital in San Luis Obispo. There, an examination showed that he had, indeed, crushed a testicle, and it was recommended that it needed to be removed. However, to have that done at French Hospital would have cost the state of California more than $10,000 in the surgical costs, the cost of the bed on the ward, nursing care and, of course, the cost of having two guards and a sergeant posted during his stay in the outside hospital. The guards would have to be posted 24 hours a day, even though he would be handcuffed to the bed.

It was decided that a CDC surgeon would perform the operation, and he would stay in the clinic ward at the prison, which saved a lot of money, especially on the guards' overtime and hazardous duty pay for hospital watch. He was very worried that something might go wrong, though some of the guys tried to cheer him up by making light of it and saying things like, 'they can't miss which one to take out, it's the one as big as an orange and flat on one side'. I went with him to the clinic, not only for moral support, but so they would know where I worked so when he was released from the ward I would come and get him. Normally they just tossed inmates back to their cells without assistance.

The day following his surgery, I was surprised to be notified about an hour after coming off the night shift at the laundry, that I could 'collect my celly'. It took me about 30 minutes to get let out of the yard.

By the time I got to the clinic door, instead of finding Jim still in the ward, he was leaning up against the wall next to where the pill call was done. He was in a heavily sedated state, holding on to a paper bag, and I could see in his eyes he barely recognised me. I got him moving back to 'A' Quad and our cell, so he could get warm and relax. He was so unsteady on his feet that I was lucky a couple of other guys helped me keep him walking. Even so, it probably took more than 15 minutes to walk him back to the cell.

After getting him settled on his bed, he fell fast asleep, something I was sure he needed. Looking in the bag he had been clutching, there were a number of pills (some for infection, and most were for pain) – but also bandages and a note addressed to me. The note was from the nurse who wouldn't hire me to work in the medical clinic when I had first arrived. She asked if I would do Jim's necessary dressing changes, as I had the knowledge, and it would save them from 'extra' work. She had put an appointment slip in for a follow-up review in two weeks, with a reminder if he had any difficulties to come to the clinic on an emergency pass.

After Jim had finally woken up and had drank some coffee and taken pain pills, I showed him the note from the nurse. He said he trusted me far more than he did the CDC medical staff. He decided he wanted to take a shower before I applied new bandages. He wasn't out of the cell for more than five minutes when everyone heard a loud scream, 'What the hell did they do to me?' I came out of the cell to see Jim wrapped in his towel heading straight for me. He ducked into the cell, with about two dozen guys looking on with confused looks. Closing the cell door, I saw him looking down where his testicles used to be. That's right, both were gone! All he had was a deflated sack. He was so angry, I thought he would have a stroke.

Jim got dressed and we both went to the sergeant's office and after explaining what had happened (Jim had to show him for the sergeant to believe us), he gave us passes to the clinic and sent a guard with us to ensure nothing got out of hand. The guard told the clinic officer that we needed to speak to the senior nurse, as she was the person that usually handled any minor complaints.

When the senior nurse came out, without waiting for her to even ask what the problem was, Jim started shouting, 'I ain't got no balls, you motherfuckers cut them both off.' The look on the nurse's face was priceless, she went completely white and even wobbled on her feet. The guard was just as shocked by Jim's outburst. After a few moments, the nurse composed herself and asked Jim to calmly explain what was wrong. I could see he was about to go on a tirade again, so I quickly spoke up and told her that he had come in for the removal of one ruptured testicle and for some reason, without even speaking to Jim, the doctor had taken both. Still shocked, she said she would look into it.

About half an hour later she came back and said the doctor's report said that when he was doing the surgery, he noticed the undamaged testicle appeared to possibly be cancerous, so he had made the decision to remove it as well. He had made a notation that he did plan to tell the patient. Jim asked for copies of all the medical records, and that included any results from biopsies and tests. The nurse said it would take a couple of weeks, but promised she would get him copies as soon as possible. When we got back to the cell, Jim took a few more pain pills than he was supposed to and went to sleep.

It was almost exactly a week when the nurse came to the cell and gave Jim the copies from his medical file. He took them to one of the inmate workers in the law library, who had been successful with winning personal damages cases for inmates against staff negligence. One of the things that helped Jim win his case and get awarded damages was the fact the CDC doctor who had performed surgery on him had been arrested driving drunk on his way to perform surgery on another inmate at a different prison. It took 18 months, and by then I was gone from CMC, but word came through the prison grapevine that Jim not only received about $200,000 in damages (his lawyer probably made twice as much), but that he was given a set of hard rubber balls implanted, so he would at least look normal. It seems that the most damning information came in a memo the doctor sent to a colleague, saying he had made a mistake and cut the wrong one off first and there was no evidence it had cancer.

When I transferred out, I was on the same bus with Charles 'Tex' Watson, someone I had rubbed up the wrong way from time to time over the seven years we had known each other. He was concerned with the move as he was going to Mule Creek State Prison, which had been turned into a 'Sensitive Needs' prison and a number of the guys sent from death row to CMC were now being sent there to protect them. I was taking the long roundabout way to Wasco State Prison.

In the first couple of years after I left, I would hear about how the CMC administration had replaced more than 800 inmates who just wanted to stay out of trouble and go home, with nearly 250 under 25-year-olds, 300-plus Northern & Southern active gang members, and inmates from Atascadero State Hospital, who were known to be violent. Within a few months of the changeover, CMC had the riots and discord it wanted, so staff could receive hazardous duty pay.

Chapter 19

A HOSTILE RECEPTION

The first time I was at DVI was in 1985. It was my third prison, having been transferred down from San Quentin after a massive 400-500 man riot at DVI. The way to try to resolve the problem was to pick 250 older inmates at SQ who stayed out of trouble and swap them for 250 young troublemakers. As I was over 30, I qualified to be sent to DVI in the hope that we could have a calming effect on the young guys. To my way of thinking, this was just a way to try to get some free babysitters and if things got worse, we would be blamed.

I had a sinking feeling in my stomach from the moment we drove out of the gate of SQ. It turned out that there would be a good reason for the feeling, because the moment we arrived in the R&R at DVI, while we were being unlocked from our cuffs, a number of the inmates working there started attacking us. About ten inmates were stabbed or slashed before the alarm was raised and the R&R officers got enough additional staff to bring everything under control. It seemed they wanted us to know we weren't welcome. They didn't seem to understand that most of us didn't want to be there either. This was my 'Welcome to gladiator school'. It was always a joke among inmates when you went to DVI that before you were released from R&R, you would be issued with a sword and a trash can lid shield.

I was initially placed in 'C' Wing. The central corridor was a bit over half a mile long. If you think that the fact that west hall, which was at the farthest distance from the main body of housing units as possible, might make this cellblock a little calmer, you are sadly mistaken. The first meal I ate in the main chow hall was interrupted by an alarm in the west hall's own self-contained chow hall. The riot ended in a couple of guys being stabbed and the rest of the inmates being pepper sprayed. In one of the other main chow halls, there was a separate incident, and we could smell the pepper spray fumes creeping into where we were eating. Some guys said it was helping the taste of the food!

The only saving grace for me was, I was given a job in the infirmary, assisting the nurses caring for any prisoners. Many would be victims of stabbings, slashings or just a simple beat down by other inmates. We had a very timid nurse, who was probably only in her fifties, though she might have been older, as she hardly talked to the other staff. For some reason she liked or, I would like to think, trusted me enough to ask if I would mind doing the wound dressing changes on the inmates who frightened her. It turned out that was just about all of them, and there were times when I would have to speak up to some of them about making comments to her which were inappropriate. Not all guys liked the fact that I would stand up to their ways, but as I had the final decision on if they got any extras like more books, a bit more food and especially one of my milkshakes, they usually realised they should be less disrespectful.

Once I had been assigned to work in the medical clinic, I had to be moved to a cell in east hall, as that is where the other inmate workers for the clinic and central corridor were housed. I was placed in a cell with a guy who had grand mal seizures. It was thought that I had the skills to be able to look after him if he had a fit. Terry was all right and very outgoing, even making light of comments made to him about the helmet and vest he had to wear, identifying his disability. He had taken a severe beating at a dorm at the California Rehabilitation Centre (CRC) over gambling debts he couldn't pay. After being in a coma for a couple of months and finally getting his seizures under some control with medication, he was transferred to DVI so he could be in a cell. You might think that experience would have stopped him gambling, but sadly not. About three months later, I was surprised to find that he had again run up substantial debts gambling and was again beaten up. This time, it was on the yard, and with weights. He did not survive. I was at my job when a guard told me to pack up his property and give it to the housing guard, so it could be returned to his family. Hours later, some of the guys who had been involved in the attack came to the cell to try to take his stuff, but nothing was left. They chose to go away as I certainly wasn't going to allow them to pressure me into paying his debts. More than a dozen guys had attacked him for more than three minutes, though only four or five were caught and charged with murder. Every one of them had gone from only doing a few years to doing life, in the blink of an eye. I found out that the debt he owed was for about $30. If prison taught me nothing else, I learned that life was cheap behind the wire. It is amazing that all who were involved in his death said in court that they only meant to scare him. I eventually ran into a couple of them years later in self-help groups, where they would speak about how they were the real victims and did not deserve a life sentence because they didn't mean to kill him. What did they think might happen when you hit someone in the head with heavy weights?

To say I was glad to get transferred out of there in 1986 is an understatement, but as with all the places I did time in, they all added a layer to make me who I am today.

I made the trip back to DVI from Folsom in 2005, and if I thought that Folsom had changed between 1984 and 1999, it was nothing like the changes I found at DVI. The most surprising was the elimination of the PIA shops, which were a mainstay at almost every prison.

In 2005, DVI was considered to be one of the better places to be and because I had worked for the captain at Folsom, he made arrangements for me to go to the DVI 'lifer unit' … though neither he nor any other staff had heard of what the unit might be.

When I left Folsom for the last time, I went on a bus with 50 other guys going off to other Level II prisons throughout California, and only three of us were going to DVI, which luckily was only the second stop for this bus. I felt sorry as some guys would be on it for up to 14-20 hours and would be having to lay over at some prison en-route before getting to their final destination.

Immediately upon pulling through the pillars, which sat on each side of the only road in or out of DVI and marked the boundary to the prison ground, I could see we were heading towards a different spot at the prison than when I arrived in 1985. Now, R&R was at the extreme west of the prison. We had only been stopped for five minutes when the R&R sergeant came out and called out the names of the three of us that were staying. We were quickly taken inside and placed in a huge holding area that could have easily accommodated 30 or more inmates. It was then I saw eight or ten inmates come out of the holding area and all head out and get on the bus, which then quickly departed.

There seemed to be only two inmate workers, but at least a dozen or more guards, which made me think, 'I guess they learned their lesson since I was last here'. The staff barely took any notice of us, though after about an hour one guard pushed a food cart towards us and gave us our dinner, which turned out to be enchiladas, rice, beans, salad and some cake, on a paper tray with a small plastic spoon. There was more than enough not to feel hungry. It was pretty tasteless, but it was at least warm. It was nearly 10 hours since we last ate.

It was more than another hour before someone came to take us down to 'C' Wing where we would be housed until we saw the classification committee. We had transferred in the bright orange jumpsuits, but it could take a few days before we would be issued our blues. I hated our travelling gear and was surprised when I came home to see so many workmen proudly wearing bright orange. I know now that for us, it was so we could be easily spotted if we tried to escape while for workmen in dangerous jobs they can more easily be found if an accident happens... I did not care for the idea of wearing the same jumpsuit for the next three or four days.

When we were assigned cells, to my amazement I was placed in the very same cell I had lived in 20 years earlier, cell 110. Inmates would say 'never write your name on a cell wall, or you'll be back to see it' but I knew I had not written my name in this cell. Same old paint on the walls, same old scratches in the door.

I had a celly waiting for me who had already been here a week and had been to committee only the day before, but was now looking to move to the 'life unit'. Samuel was unique. He was very intelligent, said to have an IQ above 160 (he was actually a member of Mensa) and probably the best chess player I ever saw in prison. I would watch him play against four guys at the same time, and rarely did he ever lose a game. However, this was our first night as cellies and as often happens, you try to get an idea of who you are sharing the 4 feet x 8 feet cell with. That means talking well into the night. Though he wasn't very outgoing, I got the feeling he was all right, just not very street knowledgeable.

The next morning, I was still in the jumpsuit and not

really happy, as Samuel had told me he had to wear his for nearly a week before they even asked for his sizes so he could be issued his blues. As we were on our way back from breakfast, I could see a number of the mainline guys in blues looking at those of us still in jumpsuits. I knew at the first opportunity I was going to remedy the problem and not do this show for the next few days, let alone a week. As we passed the dirty clothes hamper under the stairs as we headed back to our cell, I saw some blues had been tossed in there, so I grabbed up all I saw and quickly went to my cell.

When Samuel saw what I had done, he started telling me I wasn't allowed to wear blues until I had been classified. I remember smiling and telling him I had been doing time for more than 20 years, and I wasn't going to be treated like some kind of fish fresh to the line. Then I started to wash the clothes so that when we went to dinner I would be in blues and the mainline guys would have one less person to catch their interest. Throughout the day he was asking me where I had done time and, of course, the question you are never supposed to ask – 'What are you in for?' I told him how the DA of Fresno County had not stuck to the deal we made and the changes in the law that worked against me. Out of the blue he tells me he does law research and that if I ever needed help in the future, he would gladly help.

Sure enough, as we went for dinner, I was wearing my newly acquired set of blues. The guards didn't even give me a second glance, which I had been confident they wouldn't. None of them were going to actually check with the other shift or call the clothing room about it.

As I entered the chow hall, I heard some guys calling out to me, and it turned out to be those who had left Folsom on the two previous buses, a few weeks before me. Some were asking about their old cellies or friends, but a few actually asked me how I was doing and if I needed anything. They all seemed to say the same thing, 'You are not going to believe this place when you get up to L-3'. The following day right after breakfast, Samuel got the word to pack up and move to L-3. I hadn't taken notice of all the boxes of property he had until I started to help him put them on a wheeled cart. I realised how heavy they were as well. He said they were full of law books and legal work – 20 apple boxes of legal materials. He managed to get past the six cubic foot restriction (about three apple boxes) for personal property as legal materials were exempt. Samuel had very little in the way of personal clothes, opting instead to wear state-issued blues. I wasn't allowed to help at L-3, so I watched his property while he made numerous trips with the boxes. I was amazed no one came to help.

A couple of days after Samuel had left, I was called

into the classification committee. After all the usual niceties were over, it was decided I qualified for L-3 and would be put on the PIA job assignment waiting list. I had no sooner got back to my cell and locked up, when the door popped and a guard told me to go to R&R and get my property. As I was heading back to 'C' Wing, I came across a couple of guys I had known well at Folsom. They told me DVI guys didn't like the fact we came down from Folsom and caused their cellies to be shipped out. I explained that everyone who had been shipped out of DVI were Level III inmates, and we had been shipped down to give them cells at Folsom, so if anyone had a right to be pissed off, it should be us.

Back at my cell, I changed out of 'State Blues' and into my 'Personal Blues', real Levi jeans; now I was feeling better. Less than an hour before dinner, a guard told me to pack my property because I was L-3 bound. In less than a week, I had accomplished what usually took two weeks. As I was getting the first of three boxes cradled in my arms, some guys coming down the stairs from L-3 offered to help me carry my stuff upstairs, and one even took the cart back to 'C' Wing for me. This was a far cry from the reception that Samuel got when he moved in.

L-3 turned out to be a completely different type of place, even CMC. The guards were so laid back, they had inmates going behind them to get cleaning supplies out of utility cupboards. At no place or time was an inmate allowed behind staff, yet I must have seen at least half a dozen or more doing it, sometimes two at the same time.

Finally, the guards finished telling me the rules of the unit and gave me my cell key (this was only the second prison to issue me a key to my cell, the other being CMC). I found out that this privilege was only given to those who lived in L-3. Just as I walked up to my cell #345 (which would be home for the next 12½ years), who came out, but Samuel. Turns out we were to be cellies, and he seemed quite pleased about it. He explained that he had left me the bottom bunk, as he preferred the top anyway, and even got me a pillow, which was quite the luxury. I noticed we had a desk hanging down from the wall, but no seat for using it.

He said that the guy who left #345 took the stool to his other cell. It took a few minutes, but finally I got Samuel to tell me which cell the guy had gone to, and I went to retrieve our stool, as each cell is supposed to have one. As I looked in the other cell, I saw there were three stools and as the door was open a bit, I opened it up all the way and just walked in. While grabbing the nearest one, I said, 'Oh it seems someone in here accidentally took the stool from #345 when they moved, but that's all right, I'll save you the trouble of returning it'. I turned and left. I guess it took them a minute to realise what happened, as I had just stepped in my cell and set the stool down when the two guys from the other cell showed up, asking what I thought I was doing.

I could tell that neither of them had ever experienced what had happened, and not from someone of another race. In my calmest voice, I very nicely explained I understood every cell was issued one stool, and the occupants in that cell were responsible for it. As the one from #345 had 'accidentally' been removed, I was simply retrieving it, so my cell would be in compliance. One said I had no right to just walk in and take one. I explained I had been as polite as I was going to be, and if this was going anywhere else, they needed to 'Step up or step off', as I was done with their whining. It surprised me when they said I was being a bully and that's not how things are done at DVI.

This was not the 'gladiator school' I had experienced 20 years ago. Back then it would have been expected I would come for my stool, and it would have been to 'test my metal', before conceding. Unless I had received a beat down and then not only would they have kept the stool, but it would have signalled I was an easy mark.

Samuel had been playing chess when someone had told him what I had done, though by the time he got to the cell, the issue was done and dusted. He asked me what I would have done if they had both wanted to fight me. I showed him how wide the door was and explained that only one could come through at a time, so their number wasn't a factor. Besides, I didn't think they really wanted to fight over a stool, but had hoped I would give in when I saw two of them. I pointed out to Samuel that at no time did I ever allow something to be just taken from me by another inmate and to do so sets a terrible precedent, as once word gets around you are seen as weak, you become a mark to anyone trying to prove something.

I had seen it happen many times over the years. When someone allowed another to just take something small from them, a piece of cake off their tray, a cup of coffee or maybe only a pen. If the person doesn't say something, the next time it is something a bit bigger, their towel or a few soups out of their canteen bag. Again, if the guy doesn't make a point of standing up to the person, it gets worse. Next it will be someone taking his trainers (possibly right off his feet), or maybe his TV and radio. If he is still not ready to put an end to it forcibly, I hate to say it, but his protagonists will force sexual favours out of him. Once that happens, he becomes their property and they will rent him out to others, and that will be his life for the rest of his time. I did see some guys stand their ground, even if they got beat down, and more often than not, at some point he would just be left alone, and the guys would look for an easier mark.

When I first went to prison, I often turned a blind eye to things, but I saw one too many people being taken advantage of and I could see that these 'toughs' weren't all that. They preyed on the weak, usually the elderly, those with disabilities and sometimes just a young guy who had no idea what was happening but felt he needed friends. I was not the strongest or toughest, but I was often the more determined.

There was something my gunny sergeant said that carried me through life – 'You don't have to be stronger, faster or tougher than the guy you fight and most time you won't be, you just have to be the one who will go that one step beyond what they are willing to do to win'. I have been told there were times when I would get a look on my face that made others realise I might be taking something a bit more seriously than they were, and they didn't want to go there. I am not proud to say but, in a few fights, I did hurt the other guy more than I needed to, but felt that I had to make the point. It was because I had built a reputation of not necessarily starting fights, but that I would generally be the one to end them, that allowed me to stand up for guys others may take advantage of. Samuel was one of these.

It had only been a couple of days when I was approached separately by a couple of guys I had known at Folsom. Each one pointed out that by now I must realise Samuel wasn't right because of his quirky actions. He would kind of twitch and clasp his hands while grimacing, even in the chow line, as well as sitting on his bunk and rocking back and forth, to the point sweat would be pouring off him. They were offering to move in and be my celly, if I would have him sent out of the unit on a psych referral. That might sound like they were looking out for me, but in fact they were trying to watch out for themselves. Samuel and I were the only Folsom guys to be housed together; everyone else was placed in with a DVI guy who had lost a long term celly and so most of them were getting friction for it.

I didn't really care to live with either, but it was their insinuation that I would try to do something underhanded to Samuel to allow the cell opening to happen that I really found distasteful. When I explained I didn't have a problem with Samuel and even if I did have an opening for a new celly, they would not be my choices, it did not sit well with them. News got around that there was little chance to move cells, so guys started to get along and over time things mellowed out. It would be about five years before we would all be just L-3 guys.

I had to wait for a job assignment, so I used this time

to familiarise myself with what DVI was now. I learned that the gym where we had watched films before, play basketball and where there had been a few weights was now two dorm-style housing units. One half of the gym was 'Y Dorm' and the other side was 'Z Dorm' with a large corrugated fence right down the middle to separate them. 'Z' Dorm was used for those scheduled to go to the ranch, which was attached to DVI, or those just doing their short bit of time here. Even though the full name of DVI was Deuel Vocational Institution, there was not a single vocational or educational class being taught. And as there were more mainline jobs than mainline inmates, it had made it possible for reception inmates to get jobs working in the kitchen, and as porters throughout the prison. All the PIA, maintenance, hobby, library and clerk jobs were set aside for the mainline workers.

To give you an idea of the population breakdown, L-3 had 49 cells with two inmates each, making a total of 98, Z Dorm held a maximum of 250 inmates but as many would go out to the DVI ranch it was usually less than that. Then you had wings from C-J, east hall and west hall, which each held 300 inmates in cells. Due to the overcrowding, they each had about 50 inmates living in double bunks on the tier, or what was commonly referred to as the 'freeway'. That meant another 3,150 inmates. Add in the two dorms of X and Y, which each held another 250, and you have a prison population of close to 4,000 inmates – in a prison that was supposed to hold less than 1,700 maximum.

The overcrowding was not good, as it meant that the mainline and reception inmates could easily pass contraband and create 'safety and security' issues. Sadly, one of the most popular items asked for by the reception inmates was the long-handled toothbrushes we could buy in the canteen. They could only get short $2\frac{1}{2}$ inch ones. You might be thinking they wanted to take care of their pearly whites, but, no, they wanted the longer ones so they could sharpen them into stabbing weapons and could take them places such as the yard, chow hall and even church, without setting off the metal detectors. You can probably guess where they carried them so they weren't discovered during a pat down search. With multiple stabbings a day, eventually even us mainliners were only allowed the shorter ones, which the mainline population had brought on itself.

Another thing that mainline inmates lost was citrus fruit served at breakfast. You would think, it being California, that oranges would be a daily staple, but most prisons had already taken things like oranges and grapefruit off the menu. Unfortunately, it seems that the guys that came down from Folsom brought along some of the finest wine/pruno makers around, and they quickly took advantage of the fruit available, as well as the fact that the canteen sold cubed sugar and even honey. Of course, with drinking comes other problems, and a number of reception inmates in an intoxicated state began jumping on guards and other staff. So when the hammer came down on the wine producers, it came down very heavily, and some of the more serious brewers were even taken to court with new charges and collected additional sentences.

Despite the fact that at my previous prison I had held a job of some importance as captain's clerk, it was not the practice of the California prison system to consider what talents you might have before they posted you to a job in a new prison. They finally assigned me to the PIA wood shop, as a sander, being paid 30 cents an hour.

About a month later, I heard of a job opening in the administration office working for the accountant, and so I applied. Mind you, at this time all the inmates working in the offices and who held the higher pay numbers were all the DVI guys in L-3, which meant keeping the Folsom guys out on the floor of the shops at lower pay levels. Though I would find out that there was a good bit of opposition to me getting the position of account-ing clerk, the decision came down to the accountant's choice for the job, and that was me.

However, that was only my first problem. The job came with a leadman pay of 75-95 cents an hour, but some DVI guys who had been in their jobs in PIA for 15 to 20 years tried to get the PIA administrator to take that pay slot and reduce it to 65 cents an hour, so one of them could get the extra money. When I found out, I went to those who tried to pull a fast one on me behind my back and explained that if they succeeded in screwing me out of money, I would be coming to collect the difference from them. I apparently made the message clear enough because it never happened. There was so much work available, much of the time it was possible for inmates to work beyond their 6½ hour shifts to make extra money.

In the paint shop, I had become friends with the inmate leadman, who always needed extra help to fulfil the vast number of orders that came through. He allowed me to help out on overtime. I was interested in learning the powder coating techniques, as this was something I knew would be up and coming in the motorcycle industry in the free world and a skill I thought would be good to have.

I also did a brake press course, industrial maintenance course, and customer service specialist course, all with the hope that any one of them might make it easier to find a job when I got out. For nearly three years, I had worked in PIA as the accounting clerk and the inmate employability liaison (helping those who are about to be released find employment based on skills they learned in our shops), when I was notified that I had an immigration detainer placed on me and that a federal court had ordered my 'removal from the United States'. This was something I never thought would happen, and I believed it meant that soon I would be on my way back to the United Kingdom. How wrong I was on that point. All it really meant is that I would be removed from my PIA job and I would face a different type of discrimination.

Overnight, the California Department of Corrections and Rehabilitation finally 'corrected' my name to Morgan James Kane after being ordered to 18 years earlier by two California superior courts and March Fong Eu, Secretary of State for California, and notified the federal government.

That notification prompted a response within days. I had a visit from agents of the Naval Criminal Investigation Service (NCIS), the Federal Bureau of Investigation (FBI) and Immigration & Custom Enforcement (ICE), who claimed they had been trying to find me since 1997 when they were notified that the man who everyone believed had adopted me and made me a US citizen had left a dying declaration to say he had not adopted. Instead, he just used me to replace another child who ICE told me had disappeared without trace. In less than a month, I had the federal court order for my deportation.

What surprised me most was not the reaction I received from staff, but the shock of how I was suddenly treated by inmates, even ones who had known me for years. When it became common knowledge that I was a British citizen, that I had lived illegally for most of my life in the United States and when I was released I would be deported, some people became angry. With the inmates, it was either they couldn't believe what I had been saying throughout my sentence was true, or there were those who thought I had worked out some loophole to escape from doing parole in California.

There were even a few who asked me how they could become UK citizens and when I explained they had to be born within the Commonwealth or have parents who were, they often took it that I was not willing to help them, somehow keeping it a secret. I even had some staff members who thought that it was all a hoax, even with the federal government telling me I would have to leave.

The fact that I had made a good impression on the senior psychologist, Dr. S, when I took a self-help class from him, meant that when he found out I had been unassigned from PIA, he offered me a job working in the psych department as a clerk. This new assignment was by far one of the best and most fulfilling jobs I ever did in prison. It became my job to help schedule appointments for the newly arrived inmates for their first assessments with our staff psychologists and psych techs. I made it a point to keep apprised of all the rule changes at DVI concerning the reception unit inmates, so I could clarify things, especially for guys on their first trip to prison, or more importantly those that actually were suffering from mental illness.

Quite often, I would take a break from my office and go out to the fenced off areas where the newly arrived inmates waited, and speak to them through the chain-linked fence, answering questions, giving advice, but mostly just being an ear for them to talk to. As I was seen as an OG (Old Guy or Old Gangster, depending on who is using it), because of the amount of time I had already done and my age, they wanted me to reassure them that things would get better and that all was not lost. One of the biggest concerns the psychologists had was that one of the guys new to prison, and particularly with a long sentence, might want to self-harm or even commit suicide. There were times when I might notice one of them standing alone, shoulders slumped, not making any eye contact. I would always mention this to the psychologist seeing that inmate, giving them a heads-up to a possible problem.

As I did this job for more than five years, most of the staff in the psych department got to know me and that I held no loyalty to any prison group, but genuinely cared about the inmates so that, I believe, I earned their respect. This even came from the guards assigned to the area. Often when they were short-handed, I would be asked to sit at their desk and check in the inmates. There were even times, when the regular guards would be off sick or on holiday, that the replacement guards would find a note in the log book that simply read – 'Don't worry, Kane knows what to do, he will show you'. This would often shock a young guard who didn't have a lot of close contact with inmates. Two regular guards (who were classic car fanatics) even told the captain in front of me that they wanted to take me to a car rally that weekend, so I could BBQ for them. The captain looked at me and said, 'Kane, I wouldn't mind you going, but not with these two, they would likely get you thrown in prison', and they all laughed as he walked away.

While I was working for the psych department, DVI itself decided to start changing. The decision had come from CDC Headquarters in Sacramento and was well received by the prison administration, who had been wanting to move from being mostly a reception centre to having more mainline inmates. This didn't sit well with the reception centre inmates as it meant they were not going to be allowed to work in the kitchens, clothing room and as porters. Though they were not paid, they did have perks of getting extra lunches and being out of their cell, along with the possible opportunity to steal or barter to get things they can take back to their cell. The hot commodities were small radios, motors from cassette players, ink, guitar strings (to make tattoo guns out of), as well as pens and long toothbrushes for weapon stock. They were always wanting tobacco, any drugs they could get and, when possible, they were happy to get some prison wine. When the news came down that DVI would be reducing its reception centre, its inmates started to attack, not guards but any mainline inmate in blues they could, as if it was the mainliners who had proposed the change. Wasco State Prison was built to be the replacement for the California Institution for Men, which had been the reception centre for southern California. It was a long way from home for the majority of inmates finding themselves at DVI. The state also opened up small reception centres at North Kern State Prison, Corcoran, and several others to help make room at DVI for more mainline inmates.

Whenever a prison announces it is taking on prisoners due to a change in its custody level or programmes it will be offering, every other prison warden is more than willing to ship inmates to them. It should come as no surprise that the inmates being sent are not the ones who want a new opportunity to change their lives and become productive citizens upon release. Instead, every warden will be dredging up the very bottom of the barrel, every troublemaker and malcontent they want to get rid of. That is exactly what DVI got, lots of guys who would constantly be trying to get away with things, whether it was bullying, gambling, drug dealing, wine-making, or gang recruiting (we had at least 30 wannabe white shot callers arrive).

The new arrivals started right away, complaining that all the L-3 inmates had the best jobs and highest pay numbers. For whatever reason, the top officials at DVI listened, and almost overnight things started to change. Nearly three quarters of the L-3 workers for PIA were suddenly given job changes, all with a severe drop in pay and, in some cases, no pay at all. I was suddenly out of my psych clerk position and placed in the education department as a teacher's assistant. The staff in the psych department were so dissatisfied with the gang members who replaced me, they did away with the inmate positions entirely. Samuel, my celly, had been working in the library and was one of the few who did not get his job changed, as he was so knowledgeable.

The prison started to bring in vocational training programmes, but had no money to buy any actual equipment, so for nearly a year everything was done by book work alone. Many inmates assigned to the courses refused to go to them, and when you give a 25-year-old a sentence of 80 years, there isn't much incentive to programme, a point that was never understood by those who make the laws.

A struggle for supremacy started among the race groups. It began within their own groups as they established a new pecking order, then with the other races it terms of places on the yard to sit and play games (basketball, horseshoes, soccer, American football and workout areas). The newly-elected shot caller for the whites sent word up to the L-3 unit for all whites to come to the yard for a meeting with him. This sent shockwaves through the DVI guys, who had not gone to the yard in years, making their lives about going to and from jobs, chow hall, canteen and medical, with a few who only ventured out of the cells to use the toilets and shower. We had our suspicions that the majority of the DVI guys might have some special circumstances in their records that explained why they stayed here and preferred to avoid others.

On the day and time given for those in L-3 to come to the yard, none went, including myself, though my reason was that I would pick my time and not be answering to the beck and call of someone who was likely in primary school when I started doing my time. I actually waited three days, until I saw from the L-3 window that looked out on the yard, a group of about eight white guys standing around one of the concrete tables. At yard call, I left the unit to go out. Just like that, right behind me, came two other guys who had come down from Folsom. We certainly got surprised looks from the DVI guys when they watched us head down the stairs.

Coming through the yard gate, I handed my ID card to a guard, which he put in a count box. This was how they knew who was in the yard should anything happen. Stepping through the second gate, I saw one of the guards who had worked with me in the psych area. He gave me a strange look and asked if I was all right coming out to the yard, with the new mainliners on it. I just smiled and said, 'Yeah, things are just fine, just need some fresh air', as I continued onto the yard in the direction of the group I had spotted from the window. I am sure if I had looked back, I would have seen a concerned look on his face, but it wasn't him I needed to focus on, but those ahead of me. I did look over my shoulder to check the other two had continued with me and was pleasantly surprised to see they had not lost their nerve and were about 10 yards behind me.

I was still about 20 feet from the group and none of

them had yet even noticed me, deep in some mindless conversation, I was sure. I stepped right into the middle of them and said in a firm and clear voice, 'All right, who is the guy who wanted me to come to the yard?' It was as if all the air had been sucked away, nothing but silence, as I looked at each guy in the group. After a moment or so, I spoke again, 'Okay, so one of you toughs thought that I should be out here. Now I am a busy person, so how about the others pointing out who the leader is?' The other two guys had finally caught up with me, and they added their voices. 'Yeah, who is the asshole who wanted us lifers to come to the yard, well we're here'. Now the group was a bit unnerved as three guys had not only walked up on them without them even noticing, but now were demanding answers.

Finally, I caught a couple of the guys looking in the direction of one particular person and that seemed to be the signal I needed, so walking over to him, I said, 'I am Morgan Kane and I understand you have some business with me, so let's handle it'. I think the last bit of 'handle it' may have loosened up his tongue, as he quickly responded, 'No man, it ain't like that, I was just getting the keys to the car and needed to know what our numbers were'. Looking at him for a minute, I told him, 'Check this out, I don't ride in any car and unless you are going to help me get out of prison, I am going to have to assume you are going to be trying to keep me in, is that right?' I finished up with, 'If you or anyone of your motley crew does anything to try and cause me to do more time, then I will come for you personally, as I will assume either you told them to or couldn't control them, am I making myself clear?'

I could see he clearly wasn't used to being spoken to like this, and certainly wasn't expecting it from an older guy. He finally said, 'Look, I think we got off all wrong, and it doesn't need to be like this, but us whites need to stick together, don't you think?' 'No', I told him, 'I came into prison alone, have done my time alone, except when I choose to hang with someone, and I will leave prison alone, so leave me out of all your bullshit and we will get along just fine. You do understand me, right?' He looked around at the other guys who had been out there with him, and I am sure he was trying to figure out the best way out and how he could still maintain his position as shot caller. Finally, he said, 'We're all good, no problem, I'll just let everyone know you're not one of us'. I turned to walk away, but not before I looked at the other guys from L-3 and said, 'He's all yours, and I'm sure he is interested in what you have to say as well'.

As I walked away, I could hear the two of them giving the shot caller some more grief, and I noticed that about half his group had moved off, as if they didn't want to be involved if something went down. I just wished I could be left alone to get through this time the best I could. At no time could I see the need for these gangs. They do nothing to strengthen their 'race', as they claim, as it is usually their own people who they bully and take advantage of so a few at the top can have things, money, drugs and have others do their dirty deeds (such as stabbing, beating or bullying others).

It always amazed me that it was the head shot callers sitting in Pelican Bay State Prison doing 'indeterminate SHU' terms who were somehow able to make these lower-level shot callers follow their orders. No one seemed to understand that if their orders weren't obeyed, there was nothing they personally could do about it. Many people in prison who gravitate to the gangs don't do it out of loyalty to their race, they do it because they are afraid – of their gang, of other gangs, of being alone, of making decisions. Hispanic and black gang members are generally from a certain area (neighbourhood, town or county), but the whites are not, with some rare exceptions (like the Sacramaniacs, from Sacramento).

After I and the two other guys from L-3 had made it known we had no interest in being involved in whites gang politics or their problems, it came down to only a couple of the L-3 Folsom guys who decided they needed that camaraderie. One of the biggest hypocrisies I saw from the white gangs was their attitude towards other races. It was against their rules for anyone to smoke with, eat with or live with someone who wasn't white, but buying and using drugs from another race (even if it had been up their butt to get it into prison) was all right.

About two months after the new mainline arrivals started to show up, the PIA shops were shut down, without any notice, which stunned the prison population as that was where the majority of the jobs, and most certainly the best paying jobs, were. There had been no actual vocational classes now for nearly 15 years, with the only trade training coming from the PIA shops. With them gone, and nothing to replace them, as well as a growing mainline population, it was a recipe for disaster.

From time to time you might hear a rumour of someone who had run up a substantial drug debt, perhaps running into the thousands. If serious enough, that person or others might come around to try to get a donation to the 'cause' (of paying off the debt), so the person didn't get stabbed or have to request a 'lock up' for their protection. As I had made my stance on gangs and drug use well known, I was never approached for a donation, nor was Samuel as my celly.

There was one L-3 DVI guy called Short Dawg who

ran as white and claimed to be 100 per cent white, even though he was the splitting image of the actor Pat Morita (who played Mr Miyagi in the *Karate Kid* films), as he was half white and half Filipino. His half-brothers were active members in the AB and had allowed him to be 'white'. He had worked in PIA, as well as making hobby items to sell and he even tattooed, and the combined income had allowed him to stay out of drug debts. But the word around L-3 was that Short Dawg had a large debt to pay, and some guys who had lived with him for years had gone around asking for others to help. Though I liked him as a person, I chose not to involve myself, as I knew it meant me having to associate with the gangs.

One Friday night, Short Dawg received a kite (note), telling him to stand at the window at the rear of L-3 where he could see out onto the yard at 1pm yard release on Saturday. He did, but as others had got wind that something might go down, there was quite a crowd to watch. About 15 minutes after the yard had gone out and inmates were using the phones on the yard, which were right beneath the L-3 window. The 'shot caller' I had spoken to, and his lieutenant, were in a queue for the phones when eight to ten other white gang members ran up on them and started to slash and stab them. It took the guards a couple of minutes to realise what was happening and sound the alarm, while the victims continued to be viciously assaulted. The tower in the centre of the yard fired three shots in the direction of the assault, with one of the rounds ricocheting up into the wall of 'L' Block. As inmates were getting down on the yard, dozens of guards were responding with pepper spray, soaking as many inmates as possible in the area of the assault.

Some L-3 guys watching said they saw a couple of the attackers look up at the L-3 window at Short Dawg and make the gesture of drawing their thumbs across their throats and pointing at him. The next morning was Sunday, which was considered the best breakfast of the week, so most of L-3 went for it. Short Dawg was noticeably absent. We learned he had asked the guard on the unit to lock him up for his own safety, as he owed a large drug debt, and was in Ad Seg. Even though he had walked mainlines for more than 30 years on a couple of different terms, including juvenile, he could never come back to one.

Within days of the assault, the reason came to light. Apparently, the shot caller and his lieutenant (who were cellies) had racked up nearly $3,000 in drug debt owed to both blacks and Hispanics, and then had the arrogance to demand that members of their gang and other whites pay. It was decided by someone somewhere to make an example of them. It turned out Short Dawg had been their go-between, so they wouldn't be seen actually buying the drugs, and he owed more than $1,000. The other gangs had demanded satisfaction in either being paid or the debtors being dealt with by their own, or all whites would be targeted for hits (stabbings). The shot caller died of his injuries, while his lieutenant lived out his life in a wheelchair, paralysed from mid-chest down, blinded in one eye, horribly disfigured and all his bodily functions being handled with bags. Such is the glamorous life of being in a gang.

I had been cellies with Samuel for almost 8½ years (the longest time I had ever lived with anyone) and the word came down that the administration wanted to single cell L-3. Even though he had the issues with his Asperger's, he wanted to have his own cell, though I could still look out for him, rather than him moving out of L-3.

Things became unmanageable in the education department, with a new principal in charge. Teachers who had worked there for more than 20 years started to quit, which was my signal to look for a different job. Samuel and a couple of others from L-3 helped me get into the library, as the inmate disability assistance clerk, something I would find to be a rewarding job and the one I would have up until I finally paroled from DVI.

Chapter 20

THE NOT-SO-FAMOUS

During the 34 years I spent in prison, I met those who were seen as notorious or infamous, such as Charlie Manson, Charles 'Tex' Watson, Herbie Mullins, Ed Kemper and others. But there were plenty of not so famous ones. You can decide if they are good or bad, I make no judgement. The first person was not necessarily infamous outside the California prison system, but to many inside he had a bit of notoriety, and his name is Theodore Streleski.

Theodore – To outward appearances, he was a quiet, lanky, long-haired hippie type – not someone who would come to mind as a killer, yet he was. On August 18th, 1978, while a graduate student in mathematics at Stanford University, he walked up behind his former faculty advisor, Professor Karel de Leeuw, hitting him several times in the head with a ball-peen hammer. Shortly after, he turned himself over to the police. He always maintained that he believed it was a justified killing, and that he should not be held responsible, as the professor had caused him to do it. He would always state that Prof de Leeuw had denied him academic awards, repeatedly made fun of him in front of staff and students (often for wearing black and white saddle shoes with his torn jeans) and denied his requests for financial aid on numerous occasions, which he believed had forced him to leave the university, so he did not receive his degree.

Theodore had already spent 19 years trying to earn his doctorate in mathematics, sometimes having to take small breaks to work in low-paying jobs to finance his studies. At his trial, his court-appointed attorney tried to get him to plead 'not guilty by reason of insanity', but instead he entered a plea of 'not guilty'. Most damning to his defence was that he thought what he did was 'morally and logically correct' as well as it being 'a political statement as to how graduate students were treated by the mathematics department staff'. He was found guilty of second degree murder. As his crime happened before that charge carried a life sentence, he was only sentenced to seven years.

He was eligible for an earlier release, three times, yet

turned parole down each time, as one of the conditions was that he could not set foot on the campus at Stanford University.

When he was released in 1985, a few months after I had met him at the California Medical Facility – Vacaville, it is said he moved into an apartment near Stanford University, though I never heard if he ever tried to re-apply to return to his studies. It was reported in newspapers that when he was being released, he had made the comment to prison staff, 'I have no intention of killing again, though I can't predict what will happen in the future.'

Rusty – I met Rusty within days of first being received by the California prison system in 1984, and would run into him time and time again in different prisons over the years. We were together in the same unit when I was paroled. He could go from being very sociable to a total arsehole in the blink of an eye, and I came to believe he did it on purpose, just to get a reaction. What he could never figure out about me was I didn't care if he was having one of his moments and would ignore any rude comment. So he rarely had these fits of anger around me, or at least not directed towards me.

I can honestly say that I never saw, nor did he ever give me the indication, that he may have engaged in illegal sexual acts, but there were rumours. This never stopped anyone, including those who spread rumours, from going to him when they needed his expertise in fixing electrical items. To say he was good would be like saying Leonardo da Vinci occasionally painted a decent picture. Rusty was amazing. He was completely self-taught. He could fix everything from electrical cords, radios, TVs, right up to cell phones, cell phone chargers and even the guard's radios. He fixed things the prison staff would bring to him, and in return they turned a blind eye to his tools and spare parts all over his cell. He got paid in food, broken electrical things (he could scavenge from) and sometimes a new pair of tennis shoes from inmates. However, from the staff he would get food from outside – McDonald's, roast beef sandwiches, pizza and, most importantly, supplies. They would ensure he had the solder, flux, gaffer tape, superglue, resistors and fuses to help him do his work.

With more than 38 years on the inside, he stopped going to parole hearings, as he decided there is nothing on the outside to compare to his life on the inside. I will always remember him as a man who walked his own path. He was in for a first degree murder of someone who pushed him too hard and lost.

Jose – An illegal alien, a Mexican national who wanted nothing more than to farm his little piece of Mexican soil. Yet he found himself in a California prison, charged with the murder of one of his fellow villagers. He told me he had this no-nothing farm where he grew more rocks than crops in northern Mexico. His village was small, and everyone did the best they could to eke out a living. That is, until one day some guys from a drug cartel came to his village and said they wanted volunteers to smuggle drugs into America. They would give them $500 when they completed the job, and would bring them back to Mexico. Those who refused would be killed along with their family. After witnessing two men in his village killed to make the point, Jose and about six others were recruited. They were split into groups of three, taken to the US-Mexico border leading into California, given 20lbs of drugs each in a small backpack, and told once across the border to keep heading north and someone would meet them as the pack had a signal. The last thing they were told was if they failed to deliver the drugs their families would be killed.

They crossed over into the California desert and started walking north. It was July and they had no food or water, and temperatures got up above 100 degrees quickly and the terrain was rough. One of the guys with Jose fell ill from the heat, and all Jose and the third member of the group could do was try to find the sick guy some shade. The two of them decided to leave the packs with the sick guy and keep going to find the people waiting for them. They would then come back to get the drugs and help their friend. It was just getting dark when they spotted headlights on a remote dirt road and thinking it was their contact, they waved the truck down. It was only as it stopped they realised it was a border patrol vehicle, and they were now under arrest for being illegally in the country. Luckily, one of the border agents spoke Spanish, and they told them about their friend needing help and led the agents to him.

Unfortunately, the man had died while they were gone, and of course there was the issue of three backpacks full of drugs that interested the agents. They were both arrested. California Felony Murder Law states that if a death occurs during the commission of any other felony, those involved are charged with the death, even if they played no actual part in the death itself, and given 30 years to life. Jose found out that because they had not delivered the drugs, the cartel came back and killed his wife and one of his children. A brother saved their mother and his daughter, smuggling them into the US. I knew Jose for nearly 12 years, of the 27 he had done, and he was the humblest person I ever met, showing respect to everyone, with malice to none.

As an illegal alien, he could be deported back to Mexico, and this was a concern he voiced many times.

He knew that if he returned to his village, he would be killed. He saw prison as the only safe haven. He played guitar in the chapel and was a labourer for 20 cents an hour. I have the greatest respect for Jose, and he is an example of yet another victim of the drug cartels.

Big R – The crime that put Big R in jail for the last 21 years stopped being a crime 10 years ago. That's right, the crime was removed from the California Penal Code (Criminal). The charge was 'accomplice to the knowing of a conspiracy to commit an act of violence which may lead to murder or death'. It is quite a mouthful, but he was accused of possibly knowing about a conversation others had where they may have discussed doing harm to someone, and he didn't report it.

He was not actually involved with any illegal action, only that he might have known one was being talked about and did not call the police. When those who were involved were asked if anyone else was at the place at the time it was discussed, Big R's name came up. He was sentenced to 45 years to life. He made several appeals over the law being removed and yet the courts, both state and federal, have denied his plea for justice. He is still hoping his case will be reheard and he will get out, but until then he continues to play his guitar and work as a janitor in the hospital, while his wife still visits every week.

Gilbert – Here is a man who ran with the Surenos / Eme for a number of years on the streets as a teenager and continued for nearly 10 years after he came to prison. But one day he woke up and none of the gang stuff made sense anymore, and he chose to dedicate himself to the service of God. He went to the Protestant chaplain at the prison and told him that he wanted to get out of the gang lifestyle and be a more productive person. The chaplain, sensing his sincerity, gave him a job in the chapel as a porter with no pay, which meant Gilbert giving up a job that had paid him 30 cents an hour.

Now came the hard part, because he had to tell his old gang he wanted out. This was dangerous as it was not seen in a good light by the other members. Often, an announcement of wanting to quit would be answered with a stabbing. However, the shot caller had known Gilbert on the streets and realised he was willing to give up his life if necessary, to change. Having seen him give up a more lucrative job for a lowly one with no pay, decided to allow him to leave. There were three conditions. 1. He would be cut to show there was a price, 2. He could not come to them for help the rest of his term, 3. They would shun him, and he could never re-join. They gave him a razor slice across the face, and he was free of them. Gilbert walked his own path, and became a devoted worker in chapels.

Gilbert goes to the parole hearings, but believes only God will decide if or when he should get out.

Ron – This guy had some of the worst luck ever. His life of crime started in the mid-1970s with a simple burglary. He broke into a house where he 'knew' the people would be gone. But as he entered the second bedroom and bumped into the bed leg, a bedside lamp came on and a woman sat up. He had a stocking pulled over his face as a mask, and the woman screamed and then fainted away, or so he thought. He quickly ran back to the window he had used to get in with a pillow-case of items he had stolen. He went feet first to land on the ground. It seemed to work and he was soon back in his car parked around the corner, and he sped home.

Feeling he got away clean, he went to bed. Imagine how surprised he was when at 6am he was woken by police bursting through his door with guns pointing at him. They arrested him, and he was taken to the police station in just his boxer shorts and socks. He was confused as to how they had known he did the crime – he wore gloves and a stocking mask, parked his car more than a block away and hadn't told anyone. It became painfully clear how they found him, when a detective placed his wallet on the desk. It had fallen from his back pocket when he slid feet first out of the window.

They had him for the burglary, but as it was his first time he knew he would get no more than one to three years and as they got all the items he stole back, he might just get probation. Imagine his surprise when they informed him he was facing capitol murder with a chance of the death penalty. He pointed out he had hurt no one and didn't even carry a weapon. It was then explained that the woman had suffered a heart attack while on the phone to the police and the DA believed it was caused by the shock he had given her.

The trial lasted nearly two years while Ron and his attorney fought for his life. Finally, after his attorney presented statements from the victim's doctor and family all stating she had a weak heart, the attorney told him the DA was offering a one-time deal of seven to life for the murder and five years for the aggravated burglary. Ron took the 'deal'.

He had been in prison for a little over four years when he was being transported from one prison to another when the next bit of bad luck struck. He was in a transportation van with eight other inmates and just two guards, who decided to stop at a roadside gas service station / cafe to get something to eat, as the inmates had bag lunches. As one guard went to the cafe, the other allowed the inmates, who were each handcuffed and wearing waist and leg chains, out of the van to stretch a bit. Ron spotted the men's restroom and decided to use the loo. Without saying anything to the guard, fearing he would say no, Ron just went inside. With his hands chained up, it took him a few minutes, and he figured he would get yelled at when he went back to the van.

When he left the restroom, the first thing he noticed was there was no van – no van, no guards, no inmates. Apparently, they had loaded up and left him behind. As he headed into the mechanic area of the service station, he spotted a guy working there with tattoos on his neck and hands – sure signs he had likely done time – and called to him. The guy had him duck behind a truck, and then came over with some tools and got Ron out of the cuffs and shackles. He gave him an old pair of overalls and ball cap, at which point they got in the truck and the guy drove Ron 30 miles in the opposite direction. Letting Ron out, he gave him $10 and told him to keep moving until he was out of the state.

Ron did just that for two years, hitching rides with truckers or jumping on freight trains; he ate at rescue missions or stole food from stores or fields. But as he had not planned to escape, he had no idea what to do with his new-found freedom. He couldn't contact family without them being seen as accomplices. Finally, with his nerves completely frazzled from the stress and his body weakened by not eating and sleeping well, he decided there was only one thing to do and that was to turn himself in. The closest prison was California Rehabilitation Centre, and he headed there. It was early morning when he walked up to the gate and called up to the gunner in the tower. When the guard saw him, he told him to go away, and it took Ron nearly half an hour to convince the guard who he was and why he was there. Once they ran his information, a team of guards rushed out, slammed him to the ground, putting knees on his back and neck while they cuffed him up and then half-carried, half-dragged him into the prison. He had 18 months added to his sentence, as well as receiving a good beating for having escaped in the first place.

Forty years later, he is still trying to get found suitable for release and the parole board always reminds him that for two years they had no idea where he was, and can't be sure he wasn't committing crimes during that time. Additionally, over the years, he had received disciplinaries for minor offences, such as taking food from the chow hall, not walking inside a lined-off area, being late for work or just not showing up – all of these are used at the hearings to keep him in. Such is the hand he was dealt.

Samuel – My former celly had Asperger's Syndrome. He was a late life birth for his parents, who were in their early 50s. He has three older siblings, the nearest in age is 11 years his senior and the other two were more than 20 years older. He never had a close relationship with the two oldest, who were both married and practising law when he was born. He told me that they saw him as an accident or mistake, and were greatly disappointed in their parents for still having sex at that age. When Samuel was four or five his father passed away, leaving his mother to raise him alone.

Because of his condition, he was socially awkward and had no close friends, mainly only associating with his mother. Going to Catholic mass was very important to her. He managed to go to university, earning a master's degree in business administration. Not long after, his mother passed away and left his oldest brother to be the executor of her will. The death of his mother was so devastating for him that after the funeral, he disappeared from the reception and wasn't found until the following day – lying asleep over his mother's grave. His oldest siblings showed no sympathy and instead used their positions as attorneys to have him placed in a psychiatric hospital for a 72-hour check-up. The doctors could find nothing that showed he was a danger to himself or others, and he was released.

About a month later, Samuel came home to find a man in his living room, saying he had just purchased the house from Samuel's older brother, and he was giving

Samuel 24 hours to get his personal belongings out and vacate the premises. This is where the story gets mixed up between what Samuel remembers and the victim remembers. Samuel's version is that he was arguing with the man about being in the family home. Suddenly, a stranger came in the front door and started choking the victim with the tie he was wearing, until the victim was unconscious. Then the stranger ran away. Samuel put the victim in his car and drove him a few blocks to the hospital, running into the ER and shouted, 'There's a man in the car outside who has been choked'. Samuel ran back to his house and locked himself in, and that is where the police found him the following day. The victim recovered without any permanent physical injuries.

The victim's story was that he had purchased the house and had gone to see Samuel to give him notice he had to move out. At which point, Samuel grabbed him by the tie and choked him unconscious. He woke up in the hospital and told the police who had attacked him. After Samuel was arrested on attempted murder and assault, he was placed in a psychiatric hospital where he was diagnosed as being 'paranoid schizophrenic' (Asperger's was not yet a well-known condition) and he was deemed mentally unfit to aid in his defence.

For the next two years, he was forced to take psychotropic medication, sometimes being tied down and forcibly injected to make him suitable to stand trial. He was found guilty and sentenced to 10 to life. Was there a stranger, or was it a manifestation of a part of Samuel that came forth to protect him and do something Samuel wasn't able to? Samuel was my celly for 8½ years, and at no time did I ever see a violent person. He helped other inmates do their legal work and never charged. Yet the parole board denies him every time because he will not admit he was the perpetrator, and he will not admit it because he believes he is not.

On the first day, he asked me if I was afraid of wasps, and I said no. He explained that we had a wasp nest in our window and so it had to be kept shut. As I was moving my boxes of personal property into the cell, I noticed that he went out of the cell, shutting the door behind him. He had opened the window and some very pissed off wasps were flying around. I closed the window and rolled up a magazine and started killing the ones in the cell. I then got some spray window cleaner and doused the nest, killing the rest of them. I asked him why he let them in the cell. He said he was allergic to their stings and as I wasn't afraid of them, he felt I could get rid of them. That was the way Samuel thought.

Josie – Though I had met a number of queens during my sentence, Josie was one of the few I worked with and spent any time talking to. As they prefer to be addressed in the feminine form, I gave them that respect. Josie was a Sureno (Eme) and at one time went by the name of Joker. Even though she was now Josie, she was as dangerous as ever. As Joker, she had earned a reputation of being a 'torpedo', a person who carried out hits when told to by shot callers. Rumour has it, she may have been responsible for more than two dozen hits, with more than half resulting in deaths.

Josie and I worked side by side for almost three years in a prison laundry. During the wait for wash cycles to end, we had time to just sit around and talk. I told her of my background as I knew it, about being born on the Isle of Man, being brought to the US by my mother and eventually given to the man I would later find out had actually bought me. Josie told me how she had been raised by five older sisters, two aunts, her mother and grandmother and how, because she had been born male surrounded by all these women, she would get teased at school and in the neighbourhood by the other boys. It didn't help that her sisters used to dress her up in their hand-me-down clothes. After being beaten up a few times, she decided to stop it, and she obtained a 22-calibre pistol from some junkie. She walked up to the guys who had bullied her and, with a big smile on her face, she drew her pistol and fired. Six rounds found their target. Josie just turned around and headed home while reloading the gun in case she needed it.

Arrested at 10 years old for assault, as none of the victims died, though one ended up with a colostomy bag and one in a wheelchair, she was given three years in the California Youth Authority. It was there she was given the nickname Joker for the way she smiled just before getting off on someone. Being so young, different races tried to take advantage of her, including sexually, but she had the will to fight back and would stab at the slightest act of disrespect. Finally, the Surenos took her under their wing. During all this time, she played the tough boy role. Getting out at 13, and now a fully-fledged gang member, it was all about defending the neighbourhood from other gangs, retaliating, selling and doing drugs, as well as drinking. Josie had done one more CYA term and one prison term before I met her.

There came a point when Josie realised she had hidden her true identity from gang members. She had travelled to other cities to explore her feminine side and knew this was who she really was. After some soul-searching, she decided to tell her shot caller that she would no longer be Joker, but was now Josie. He took it better than she expected, though some guys weren't so accepting. She explained she did not want to leave the gang, but just be herself. To prove she was still loyal, the shot caller gave her a hit on a high-ranking member of a rival gang. So dressed up as a seductive woman, lured the target from a safe zone into a back alley and stabbed him to death. She was only caught when one of her own gang became a police informant and gave up the weapon with Josie's fingerprints on it, along with guns and drugs belonging to the gang. Josie and about half a dozen others were arrested on numerous criminal counts, with the majority ending up with life sentences.

Josie made no excuses for what she did. She was always very matter of fact. You could never imagine the violence she could wield. She was paroled a few years before me, and I heard she had the full gender re-assignment and is married to a bank manager.

Jim – He was the luckiest person when it came to gambling, and it wasn't just at cards, which he rarely seemed to lose at. Even in chess games or betting on football and basketball shown on TV, he had a 75 per cent win rate. Before he came to prison, he had been a pool hustler, making a living travelling around America, playing high stakes games and tournaments, sometimes worth up to $100,000. He would be hired to play by wealthy types and get about 30 per cent of any pot he won by beating whoever was put up against him.

At birth, he had been the victim of his mother taking

Thalidomide during her pregnancy, and so Jim had been born with a shrunken left arm with only two fingers and a thumb. It was this condition that he believes led his mother to give him up for adoption, something that never happened because of his disability. It also earned him the disrespectful name from other inmates of 'Chicken Wing', which he was called, even by staff.

As he grew up in the California foster system, he moved homes and schools on average three times a year. His physical condition did not make it easy to fit in. Jim took to cutting school and hanging out in pool halls perfecting his craft of hustling. It was because of one of these high-stake games that he found himself in prison.

In a seedy part of Sacramento, he had been invited to take part in a game that had a $500,000 purse, six players each putting in $100,000 (the house got the extra $100,000 for providing the venue). It came down to just Jim and a local guy named Jake, who was a bully. After four games of five, they were tied and the tension in the air could be cut with a knife. Jake had the table and only had to put away his last two balls and the eight-ball to take the pot. Jim had four balls still on the table. But Jake had been drinking, although it was his arrogance that was his undoing. As he lined up his last run, out of the corner of his eye and giving Jim a smirk, he hit the cue ball slightly off the mark and missed the shot. This allowed Jim to take to the table and win the $500,000. But when Jim was collecting his money, Jake pushed him down and took it from him, saying, 'I ain't losing to no crippled-up freak'. Witnesses would tell the police they saw Jake leave by the back door to the alley, and moments later Jim grabbed a Jack Daniel's whiskey bottle and went after him. An hour later, as someone was taking out the trash, they found Jim laying in a crumpled heap with a knife in his side and a few feet away lay Jake with his skull caved in, and the whiskey bottle embedded in it.

Both were taken to the hospital. Jim survived, Jake did not. Jim was charged with aggravated battery and second degree murder. The money was never found. Jim was sentenced to 21 years to life and died during his 27th year in prison from Hepatitis C, it is believed he caught from drug use.

Finn – Here was a guy who had the world at his fingertips. He had been a third generation firefighter from an old Irish family. His career had taken him to the position of arson investigator and he was respected by not only members of the fire department but also the judicial department in Los Angeles County. His investigative skills and testimony had solved many fire-related cases that had perplexed other investigators. Unfortunately, he, himself, was arrested for committing arson. Initially, he was arrested when he had appeared on CCTV at one of the crime scenes, leaving just before the fire started.

When questioned, he stated he had no memory of the event and had been suffering headaches. Before he went to trial, he was given a full medical examination, which revealed he had extremely low lithium levels. It was believed that this chemical imbalance was the likely reason he may have committed the act he was charged with and had no memory of it. Because of his excellent work record for the fire department, it had been recommended that he be given a two-year suspended sentence, which would be expunged if he committed no more criminal acts, and that he had to undergo treatment to raise his lithium level. In the meantime, he had been removed from being an active member of the fire department. For Finn, this was a terrible outcome, as all he had ever wanted to be was a firefighter and to be of service to his community.

He now found himself with a job working in a men's high-end retail shop. Though he still saw some of his old fire-fighting buddies, he knew that until he was able to work with them again, he would not be happy. As soon as the two years were up, he enquired about being able to work for the fire department and was told that as long as he took the lithium medication it would not be possible as it would make him heat sensitive. He stopped taking his medication and started hanging out in a bar where the fire-fighters would gather.

No-one could say for sure what happened, but almost three months to the day after he had stopped taking his lithium, he killed a man in the bar with a broken beer bottle. He was sentenced to 17 years to life for a second degree murder. The problem that he started to have when he became eligible for a possible parole date was the question posed to him by the parole board, 'How can you guarantee us that you'll never stop taking your lithium medication at any time in the future, if we release you?' He could give them no answer, and 36 years later he is still doing time.

Moose – This guy had been my celly for about a year, and we spoke a lot about what we had done before prison. He had only graduated from high school a few months earlier. He was one of those jock-type guys who could play all competitive sports, though he had excelled in both football and baseball. Moose's mom had polio when she was a young girl and was in a wheelchair, but she adored Moose as he had been the dedicated son who was always there for her.

A month after graduating, Moose and about 40 of

his friends had a house party to celebrate. A few people who had not been invited decided to crash the party. One was the football coach's son who, though he was the equipment manager for the team, had no athletic ability. Once at the party, he started harassing some of the girls about going off with him. When Moose saw this, he confronted the guy and told him to leave because he was drunk. The guy replied, 'Okay, I'll leave, but I'm not afraid of you and next time I see that crippled mother of yours, I will dump her out of her wheelchair.' To which Moose responded, 'If you ever touch my mother, I will kill you.' This statement was made in front of everyone at the party.

It was less than a week later that Moose took his mother shopping. After letting her out in front of the store, he went to park her disabled van. The guy Moose had argued with was coming out of the store, drunk and carrying a six-pack of beer. When he saw Moose's mother sitting by the kerb, he grabbed her wheelchair, and tipped her out of it. Moose saw this happen and, running to his mother's aid, he righted her wheelchair and lifted her back into it. The guy said, 'I told you I would do it, now what are you going to do?' Moose responded with a single punch to the guy's chin, causing the guy to fall to the ground, hitting his head on the kerb.

By the time the police arrived, the guy had died from

that one punch. Moose was arrested and even though all his friends at the party spoke on his behalf about the other guy's threat, the most damning thing was when they related in court that Moose had warned the guy that if he carried out his threat, he would kill him. Initially, the jury found Moose guilty of only involuntary manslaughter. However, the prosecutor was able to appeal the conviction and get a higher court to find him guilty of second degree murder, which gave him 17 years to life. His mother never missed coming to see him every month for the rest of her life, no matter which prison he was in. She died 15 years ago. Moose died one day after her, committing suicide when he was given the sad news of her passing.

Russ – He was a member of the class of '76, which was the term given to those who had been on death row between 1972 (when the death penalty was first declared unconstitutional) and 1976 (when it was again struck down, having been reinstated in 1973). Russ had been an independent photographer in San Francisco, doing mostly layouts for ads for magazines. These photo shoots were almost entirely of young ladies. A friend he knew in the San Francisco Police Department, asked if he could take some photos at a crime scene for them.

He described his first murder scene as extremely

brutal. He did about a dozen scenes for the San Francisco PD when they offered him the job of official photographer. Not only was he on their payroll, but, more importantly, he would be given an 'official' San Francisco Police Department ID card and badge. At no time did they ever do a background check on him. If they had, they would have seen he had been incarcerated as a teenager for 'sexual misbehaviour' in another state. There were more than a dozen counts, stemming from taking photos up women's skirts. He served six months on a youth farm. He used to joke about it being harmless fun when he talked about it during a self-help class. Sadly, about half the other guys thought it was, too.

The fact he had official ID documents allowed him access to closed case files and evidence held at the police department, which he often viewed under the guise of 'research'. Something unlocked a secret and sadistic desire in Russ. He started to pay college age girls to model for him. These special sessions would consist of the girls being scantily clad and, more often than not, placed in bondage situations, as these photos were being sold to 'men's' magazines. Russ would be paid quite well. He kept this part of his life separate from those friends he had in the police department.

He had been working with the police for nearly three

years and his excellent eye in taking the photos often identified pieces of evidence that had been overlooked, which aided the prosecutors to get convictions. It may have been an ego thing with Russ, but in the group therapy sessions, he would often brag about how most of the girls he photographed would come onto him. Most guys on the prison yard saw him as a lecherous troll when he would talk about how he posed the girls, and figured he was the one making advances. The reason he killed the girl he was initially arrested for was that he owed her money for a photo shoot, and when he refused to pay, she threatened to go to the authorities and tell them what kind of photos he was taking. Realising that his friends on the police force would not approve, he saw a bleak future if the information got out. He would tell people that she died when they were struggling. What he didn't figure on was that the girl had told some others at her college about her dealings with him, and that she was concerned about confronting him over the money.

When she didn't turn up at school, they called the police. At his studio, the police found Russ had thousands of photos of girls in compromising bondage poses, as well as a room where bondage equipment was kept. It was the nailed-shut closet that drew their attention most. They found the dead girl's body wrapped in thick plastic sheeting and sprinkled with lime dust. During the investigation and trial, they identified 20 other girls from photographs who had been reported missing. With the photos and the multiple bags of lime they found, though circumstantial evidence, when that was added to the one deceased girl, a jury found Russ guilty on one count of murder and 20 additional counts of complicity in the disappearance and possible deaths of the other girls, for which he received the death penalty.

It wasn't him killing the girls that gave him problems in prison. The fact he had worked with the police and prosecutors in San Francisco meant other inmates disliked him. Because he had been given the job of inmate yard photographer, most guys only dealt with him to get a photo to send to their families or as the parole board required. While he was relatively 'safe' at the California Men's Colony, in 1993 he was notified he would be transferred out to one of the more unsettled prisons. He feared for his life as he knew that at any other prison, the fact he worked for the police would likely be a death sentence, something he had beaten when the court had changed the law in 1976, He thought he had found an ingenious solution. He made the excuse that he needed to take a photo of an inmate who was dying of AIDS in the prison hospital. When he got there, he managed to get some of the guy's blood and injected himself. He knew if someone was diagnosed with HIV or AIDS they would not be transferred.

He was placed in isolation until they could prove he was infected. He hoped they would find a treatment or a cure for AIDS in just a couple of years. But in 1996-97, I heard that he had died due to complications from AIDS. I know of no one who shed a tear for him.

Mikey – Here was an 89-year-old guy who used to argue with the parole board. They suggested he take vocational training courses, so he would have some skills to gain employment upon his release. He would always point out that he had been retired for 10 years before coming to prison and that he had no intention of doing any kind of work, if released. Mikey had been in prison since he was 75, for 'criminal aiding in the death of another', which is what assisting in a suicide was called. He had been 16 years old and his wife was 15 when they married in 1917. He was an apprentice blacksmith during WWI and then worked for an aircraft manu-facturing company, becoming a mechanical engineer. Finally, he owned his own manufacturing business until he retired. His wife, unfortunately, had been stricken with cancer that had ravaged her body and had spread into her brain and bones. He had been dedicated to her for more than 60 years and they had four children.

Even though she was on strong painkillers, including morphine, she would cry when he held her. He had watched her deteriorate from a vibrant partner to a very thin and terribly ill person for whom no relief or peace was available. After this progression into despair, finally he could no longer ignore her pleas to 'let her go'. He made the decision to help her. He prepared her medication as usual, but more than tripled her dose of morphine. As they lay in bed together and shared a glass of wine, she took her medication. In a short while, she drifted off. Even after her last breath, he held her for more than four hours before calling their eldest son, who was a doctor. When his son arrived, he confessed what he had done to help her alleviate her suffering.

His son called the police and became the primary witness against him at trial. Yet his other three children rallied to his defence. He was found guilty and given 10 years to life sentence. At his last parole board hearing, the commissioner had made the suggestion that Mikey should think about taking an underwater welding course, to which Mikey responded, 'Maybe you should see a doctor, so you can get your head out of your arse.' At the parole board's suggestion, he was transferred to Tehachapi State Prison, which sat up in the hills and was known for heavy snow. Inmates had to walk from their housing units outside to get to the chow hall, even if it was raining or snowing. It was during a trek for a meal in three feet of snow during his first winter there that he succumbed. He was found, lying dead with fresh snow falling on him. He never saw 90, but in a moment of reflection, I would hope that he is with his wife.

Sea Hag – A merchant marine during Korea, he later spent more than 20 years working on commercial ships, which is how he picked up his nickname of Sea Hag. He had developed a reputation for being a brawler, and he was not known to have shied away from a confrontation, no matter how serious it might be. He would be the first to admit that his great love of the sea had broken up his marriage. He never remarried, and was always there for his ex-wife, and especially his daughter. Sea Hag was in prison because of an incident involving his daughter and two of her friends. During one of his trips back from overseas, his daughter confided that she and her two friends had been physically touched by some men who lived in a halfway house near her school. Even though she had told her mother, who had reported it to the police, nothing had been done.

Sea Hag went to the house and spoke to the psychologist who ran it. He was told the men who lived there were recovering paedophiles who had volunteered to participate in an experimental programme to try to make them less dangerous. Each of the men in the house had been convicted of at least one sexual act against a child. Sea Hag said that the psychologist told him there was no guarantee that any of them could ever be truly cured as paedophilia was a mental health issue and these men needed sympathy for their suffering.

Sea Hag then went to the police to express his dissatisfaction with the investigation, and shared with the senior detectives what the psychologist had told him. One of the detectives made an off-hand comment that if it had happened to his daughter, he would just kill the bastard. Sea Hag said that he thought he had just been given permission to become the cure for their illnesses.

Later that day, he went to a gun shop and purchased a Mossberg 500 8-shot riot shotgun and a box of 20 shells. He drove back to the halfway house and sat outside waiting to see them sit down at the dining room table, which was visible from the street. It was just about 6.30pm when he observed a number of men having their dinner. He calmly got out of his truck with a loaded shotgun under one arm, spare shells in his jacket pocket, and walked up to the front door and kicked it open. Stepping into the doorway that led to the dining room, he started firing the pump-action shotgun in the direction of every person there. Once he had emptied the eight shots, he reloaded and started walking through the house looking for more paedo-philes. He had shot and killed seven in the dining room, and as he was leaving two more were walking up, and he killed them on the sidewalk before getting back in his truck and going to his ex-wife's house. He had told her what he had done, and that their daughter and her friends would no longer be bothered by these men. What he didn't know was that the psychologist and a tenth paedophile he was counselling had fled out of the house through a back door when they first heard him start shooting. They saw him drive away, taking down his licence plate number and description, which were given to the police, who arrested him later that evening.

Sea Hag would tell anyone who asked that, yes, he had done the crime, and no, he had no regrets. He had gone with a 'trial by judge' rather than jury. Instead of being given the death penalty, he had been given nine life sentences running consecutively, what we in prison would call running bow-legged. This meant he would have to be found suitable and released from one life sentence before starting the next one. In reality, he knew, just as the rest of us did, that he would never see the outside world again. One of the greatest joys that Sea Hag had was that his daughter and her two friends would visit him, and his daughter made sure that his two granddaughters got to know what a wonderful, loving father he was. He worked as a clerk and built historical clipper ships out of lolly sticks as a hobby. He took the time to make them look as realistic as possible and would sell these for thousands of dollars. Two of them had found their way to the governor's mansion in Sacramento.

He also participated in two clubs. The first was stamp-collecting. The second and more important one, was an investors club, which was sponsored and run by the outside investment firm, Blakeslee and Blakeslee. All the money that Sea Hag earned from selling his model ships and his pension, he placed into stocks and bonds. When a new guard started making rude comments about his hobby and how someone who had committed such heinous crimes should not be allowed to be a building clerk, Sea Hag calmly walked to his cell, picked up a file and slapped it down in front of the guard and told him to open it. The moment the guard looked at the very first page, his eyes got wide and his mouth dropped open and he went pale, which caused Sea Hag to smile.

Sea Hag then told him, 'I have a $2.5million stock portfolio that will go to my two granddaughters when I die, so they will want for nothing.' He added that he was worth more after being in prison for 20 years than the guard would ever be worth, and 'I'm only half the arsehole you are'. Sea Hag was one of those men who was straight with you. However, if he thought you were out of line, he would point it out to you. He passed away nearly 10 years ago, but I know for a fact that even if he knew what the outcome of his actions would be, he would still have done it anyway.

Jody − My little Irish friend helped to teach me more Gaelic. He was always up to mischief, but he was never out-and-out mean, though the few times I saw him threatened, he would throw down quickly to let the others know he was serious. He was one who had my back, and he knew I'd be there for him. He had come from Ireland as a young man, and because of a girl, he joined the US Marines. Though he lost the girl, he did get the right to stay in America, which I think was his plan all along.

The biggest problem he had was that he liked other people's things. He stole nice cars and had carried out the odd burglary. He was not very good at either and was always caught, getting a year or so each time. When I met him, he had taken a truck fitted with a tracking device and, as luck would have it, he was stuck in traffic with a police car behind him when it came over the police radio. He swore that was to be his last act of criminal behaviour, as it didn't seem to suit him. He was a decent guy, though he was a diabetic, and a bad one at that. Jody would eat everything he wasn't supposed to and couldn't be bothered to exercise any more than the walk to the chow hall and back, or out to the card tables on the yard and then back to his cell.

He loved to tell stories and jokes about growing up in Ireland. He would speak with such passion, and you could see the joy and sadness in his eyes when he spoke of his mother. I only knew him for the 18 months we were together at Folsom, and he kept in touch for six months after he had been released. Then I received a letter, not from him, but from his brother telling me that Jody had passed away from complications due to his diabetes, after having fallen into a coma. He used to brag that he had a girlfriend who worked at Starbucks and she would bring him home those really sweet and chocolatey coffees. I think I was more surprised that it had not happened sooner, considering how poorly he took care of himself. What many may not have known, including his family, was that he had stopped caring about his health after his mother had died a few years earlier. He regretted he was in prison when it happened and he wasn't able to go to her funeral. His brother told me that the family was taking Jody home to Ireland to be laid next to their parents. In the end, Jody got home and was able to be with his mother once again.

Chapter 21

THE LONG ROAD TO FREEDOM

You may be wondering why so many of the men I have described, including myself, serve such long sentences, some to the point where they decide they might as well spend the rest of their lives in prison. We were lifers, dependent on the whims of the parole board. These boards are the most trying of interviews anyone might attend. With each one you are really fighting for your life, and although there is supposed to be a set format, I have never seen one that followed the same pattern.

Originally, the parole board panel was composed of three members, one of whom was supposed to be a member of your previous panel. This was to ensure a fair hearing because that member could relay to the panel whether the inmate had carried out the recommendations of the previous panel. As time passed the board was reduced to two, but not until my ninth, and very last hearing, did I ever have a member of the previous panel in attendance. I appeared before nine different sets of board commissioners, and each set never cared whether I had done what the previous board had asked to ensure my release. Generally speaking, they liked to point out that I had not met their standard to be found suitable for parole. It was as if the board deliberately changed what was wanted from you each time, in order to make you fail. My experience was mirrored by thousands of other inmates.

But how did one get to the board in the first place? There was a point in the sentence when parole could be considered. Through Californian legislation, that date lengthened considerably since I started my sentence in 1984. I had been given a 27 to life sentence, and as I earned half time credits for work and behaviour, I was supposed to go to my first board in 1996, so that I would get out in 1997, in keeping with the 13 years I had been promised I would serve. However, the law changed in 1989 and all good/work time credit was taken away, so my first eligibility for parole became 1999. When I had served 25 years.

Even before going in front of the board, certain formalities had to be observed. First, your counsellor, who you might only see once or twice a year, sets up a report for the parole board to read. It includes the DA's version of your crime, plus what you have told the counsellor about it, your behaviour in prison, and your educational, vocational and work reports. Yes, whatever you do is reported on every step of the way, including the all-important self-help chronos, any involvement with gangs, your reported parole plans if released, and finally their recommendation on whether they think you should be released. You are supposed to get a copy of their report a week ahead of your board, but we considered ourselves lucky if we received it three days ahead. Generally, you only got to see it a couple of hours before you went into the hearing. Considering that you could only dispute any of its contents at the board itself, they weren't allowing you much time for preparation.

The next pre-board hurdle is the notorious forensic assessment and diagnostic report or FAD, which is done six months before your date, by a parole board psychologist, who, having never seen you before, interviews you for three to six hours. You are supposed to get a copy of the report three months prior to your hearing, but although you can dispute his findings, your opinion carries very little weight with the board.

The board is also supposed to read through a whole range of information that the department of corrections and rehabilitation, the district attorney and various victims groups, has assembled. A lot are documents you have never seen, as they are kept in the confidential part of your prison file. It was not until my failure at my seventh board that my attorney was so enraged by the decision that he grabbed some of these 'secret' papers that had been left for the district attorney, and we discovered that all my past boards had been relying on information that was a pack of lies.

In fear and trembling of how they can make or break your life, you eventually meet at the appointed hour, possibly as early as 8.30am, with a board now armed with the information they have assembled on you.

So who are these people, the board? In California, the law says that the parole board is a cross-section of society. Except for the odd person from the education field or a psychologist, the majority of members are ex-law enforcement, DAs and victim rights advocates. So yet another hurdle to get over.

The hearing starts with the usual explanation of what the board has allegedly done in preparation, and whether you understand what is going on and what the purpose of the hearing is. They then move onto pre-commitment factors, which you do not become aware of until long after the board, when you get their version of the transcript.

The board does not just discuss the crime for which

you are in prison, but they take into account every other offence you might be guilty of, right back into your childhood, regardless of how long ago that might have been, how much reparation you made and whether that past offence had any connection in any shape or form with the crime for which you are now serving time. There was nothing in the first 25 years of my incarceration where it was a requirement to express and explain 'insight and remorse'. That is, until a parole board member coined the phrase, and then it became the rallying cry by all panels, DA representatives, appellate courts and victims' groups. Now, everyone has to express remorse, whether they feel it or not. Strangely, I did feel remorse about the death of the victim in my case, although I was not personally responsible for killing him. That is, up until the summer of 2011, when I was handed a copy of the statement from the man I believed had adopted me, in which he admitted he had paid the man who died to come to Fresno to 'do me harm'. I now realise the unexplained faults I had when riding my motorbike, any one of which could have killed me, must have been his doing and not my bad workmanship. I found it more and more difficult to be sorry that he was dead. But in order to get parole, that was a thought to keep to myself. Insight and remorse are subjective concepts that have different meanings and scales to different people. So one board member might believe an inmate is expressing genuine remorse and showing full insight, the next will find none at all. That variation is frustrating to the inmate trying to understand how to express both.

Then they look at post commitment factors, which is your behaviour within the prison system. In theory, they are only supposed to look at your conduct since the date of your last board, but, in fact, they look back over the last 15 years or three boards, whichever is the longest. That means that if you have got the blame for a fight you were in 15 years ago, it would be a reason to refuse parole. They would also want to know how well you had 'programmed'. That is going to classes, whether vocational or self-help. But when someone is sentenced, it is stated that they should be removed from society for a specified period. Nowhere in the court's transcript does it say that the person has to complete any education, vocational or self-help programmes in order to be found suitable for release.

The system cannot rehabilitate anyone, all it can do is provide the tools to allow a person to rehabilitate themselves and, yes, the system can offer encouragement. However, the worst travesty is when someone has spent years taking courses and trying to better learn what goes on inside them only to be constantly denied by the board panel, who then asks for more from them in the future.

Having got over all the parole board hurdles, there is one last mountain to climb. The governor of the state of California has four months after the date of your parole in which he can override the decision and deny you parole.

I have sadly watched guys just give up on performing for the parole board, choosing to stay in prison. Some guys who were finally granted parole 35-50 years after they went in decided there was nothing outside of prison for them and declined to leave, even if it meant they had to catch a disciplinary to have their parole revoked.

To give you some idea of the vagaries of the parole boards, here is what happened at the ones I was obliged to attend. Remember, I did not actually commit the crime, murder, for which I had been sentenced. In 1984, I took a plea-bargain for a crime that I believed my then wife had committed, in order to save her from a death sentence.

1999 – This was my first chance at possibly being released, and I had a panel made up of three men. As it had been a state appointed attorney that helped me get into prison, I didn't think I could take the chance to have one represent me at this hearing, so against the advice of the prison staff and some inmates, I chose to represent myself. I thought that having taken every course on offer to upgrade my job skills, they would have no choice but to find me suitable. I had participated in a couple of dozen self-help therapy programmes, and had a number of letters of support from people out in the community offering me jobs and housing help upon my release. The hearing lasted nearly three hours and there was no representative from the district attorney's office to sit in opposition, nor did they send a letter (part of the plea-bargain deal I had taken was they would never oppose my release). I had four psychological and risk assessment reports, with the newest one being only six months old. Each of them, done by different psychologists, gave me a listing of being a 'low risk to reoffend', with my latest one saying, 'He is less violent than the average inmate and no more violent than the common man on the street'.

Yet even after all the evidence had been laid out and discussed, the commissioners had concerns. I was told that 'I had done too much, and it was giving them a problem in finding a reason to deny me'. They went on to explain about the political climate, that the governor of California, Gray Davis, was still following the 'no parole' policy for lifers, which his predecessor Pete

Wilson had put into place 15 years earlier. I asked that they allow me to fight the governor in the courts if he chose to take my date. They said they felt they were doing me a good turn by denying me now and when I came back, with luck, the political climate would have changed in my favour. I was then denied for three years for the only reason they could find, 'gravity of the nature of the crime'.

2002 – At my second chance for parole, I appeared before two female panel members. Again, there was no letter or representative from the Fresno district attorney's office to oppose my release. This time, the psychologist's assessment stated, 'I agree that he does not have a potential for re-offense or violence in the community at this stage in his life and is seen as a low risk in comparison with other inmates'. Yet, to my amazement, this board were more concerned that once again I had chosen not to be represented by an attorney, even to the point of chastising me for not being sensitive to the fact that being a board attorney was a thankless job and didn't pay much, so I was denying the attorney the opportunity to feed their family. After two hours of telling me I had to stop being so selfish and needed to put others' needs before mine, they denied me for three years. Their reasoning was that they felt I had been 'performing too well and believed it was only to impress them'.

2005 – My third hearing was supposed to be held at Folsom, but I transferred back to Deuel Vocational Institution when I was under the 90-day window (which was against their rules), so my hearing was held six months late. Though the commissioner was a seasoned veteran, he allowed the newly assigned deputy commissioner to run the hearing. This was a bit distressing as the deputy commissioner proudly stated in his opening comments that I was one of the first inmates to come before him, and he hoped that I may be willing to forgive any error in my hearing, or any decision he made concerning me being found suitable. This did not fill me with a lot of confidence that I would be given a fair hearing. The commissioner said nothing to me, except to introduce himself before the hearing and wish me good luck after they denied my parole. Throughout the three-hour hearing, the deputy commissioner would constantly avoid asking me about the positive things I had accomplished in prison, choosing to focus on what I had done 23 years earlier, before I had been arrested. Things like why I rode motorcycles, which he saw as anti-social behaviour, and telling me that he was sure that if I lived that lifestyle, I must have used drugs and abused alcohol. When I denied it, he would become even more insistent that I was lying. He explained that he had been a deputy sheriff for more than 20 years and had never known a biker who didn't do drugs and alcohol to excess.

This was the first time a representative from the Fresno district attorney's office showed up and openly opposed me. When I tried to point out that in the deal I took, the DA said they would never oppose it, the representative said, 'There is now a new district attorney who was not a part of that deal, and he is opposed to anyone from Fresno County being found suitable or released.' He did point out to the panel that I had done nearly two years in the Alcoholics Anonymous programme while I was at CMC. I told the board I was advised to join, although I had no history of alcohol abuse. I showed them a copy of the chrono I received when I left the group and they were gobsmacked! They could not believe it. At this board, I did take a state appointed attorney, who sat through the whole hearing without saying anything except to give his name for the record. Not once did he object to anything said to me. Once the panel came back from deliberating my future, the deputy commissioner stated that he didn't think I truly understood the gravity of my situation, so he didn't feel comfortable in finding me suitable for parole.

They recommended I spend less time developing work skills and focus more on reflection by way of self-help classes, then added I needed to stay disciplinary free and get positive chronos. Finally, they said they weren't sure what the psychologist meant in his report that 'I had the ability to make even more positive changes once I was released into a free society'. They gave me my first two-year denial based on them believing me to be 'an unreasonable risk to society if released on parole'.

2007 – I believed that I had met all the criteria set down by the three previous hearings and should be found suitable. I had been given a pen pal by Prisoners Abroad in 2006, and they urged me to accept a state appointed attorney. The week before my hearing, he finally showed up. With his feet up on the table in the attorney visiting room, he looked me in the eye and said, 'I really don't know what I can do for you, and you have to understand I personally only do this job for the easy money and hope most of you guys don't get out'. You can't imagine the look on his face when I picked up the board file he had been given and told him 'not to show up at my hearing as I would be representing myself'. He tried to get the file back and even called for the guard, but when I told the guard, who happened to have worked as my tier officer, what he had said, I was allowed to leave with the file. I could tell right away that the panel was not happy that I was not represented by legal counsel, and my explanation as to why I fired him at the last moment concerned them as well. They even offered me the right to postpone my hearing to a later date, when I could get another attorney, yet even this was not in my best interest, but actually theirs. To ask for a postponement, you had to sign a statement that says 'I do not feel I am suitable for parole'. This is a double-edged sword. Not only do you have to wait another year to come back, but the next panel will want to know what makes you think you are now suitable. I told them I was fine and ready to proceed.

Once again it was a two-man panel, and the hearing was only about two hours, my shortest to date. Though there was no air of arrogance from the panel, the representative from the DA's office tried to make it seem that I was by far the worst person who ever walked the earth. He even used the fact that I thought I was qualified to represent myself as a sin. He made the foolish mistake of asking me why I resisted becoming a part of 'normal' prison society. I responded by saying, what did he find normal about being in a gang, selling and using drugs and bullying weaker people. I then made the mistake of asking him, 'How many times did you get your milk money taken in school and is that the reason you became a prosecutor, to get back at those who bullied him?'

I realise that saying something like that to the DA representative was not a smart thing to do in front of a parole board panel, yet I felt the need to bring him down off his god-like perch. You could usually feel how the hearing was going about a third of the way through, and I knew this one wasn't going in my favour. Though the panel was only mildly adversarial, they made comments about courses and programmes I had not taken that they knew other inmates had participated in. Again, they did not appreciate me telling them that those programmes were not available at the prisons I had been at. They even asked why I had not asked to be transferred to prisons with programmes available. I had to point out to their amazed and confused faces that in most cases the programmes were at prisons that were either above or below my custody level, and besides, the California department of corrections did not generally move an inmate to a prison of their choosing.

Even having been given a 'low risk' assessment again, the panel found me 'unsuitable'. They felt I had 'programmed in a limited manner and that I did not meet the standard they felt necessary to be found suitable'. I was given a two-year denial and with their wishes of good luck, I was sent on my way. It was this denial that so incensed my pen pal that she suggested I try to return to the UK under the International Transfer of Prisoners Treaty. It was my application which forced the US Immigration and Customs Enforcement (ICE) to visit me and inform me that instead of having dual nationality as I thought, I had never been adopted legally and was therefore an illegal immigrant.

2009 – At my fifth parole hearing I had another dump truck state attorney, who did not even bother to show up until 10 minutes before the hearing and hadn't even read my file. He said not to worry, as he was used to 'just winging' these things. The panel was one man, who had been the deputy commissioner in 2005, and one woman.

Initially I had a good feeling as I had accomplished everything he had asked for in his 2005 hearing. It had only been a year before that the state of California finally decided to follow, not just two court orders, but also one issued by the California secretary of state, ordering that all my prison records and my ID card should reflect my birth / legal name of Morgan James Kane. From the beginning of this hearing, it was made clear I was not to be referred to in any other manner. If he did nothing else, the state-appointed attorney had accomplished that feat. This hearing did not go off without a hitch, though. It had been scheduled to start at 8:30am, but the DA representative did not arrive on time, so I was kept waiting for another hour. He still hadn't shown up, so the parole board panel elected to start the hearing. I took this as a sign that things might work out all right this time, especially when I realised that the commissioner had removed his jacket and seemed to be quite relaxed, which was certainly not the norm for these types of hearings.

The commissioner was interested about the time since our last meeting. He even joked with the deputy commissioner that I had been one of the very first hearings he did, and that he had been amazed at my life story. The mood was very light and without tension. After the hearing had been going for a little more than an hour, the DA representative arrived. After making a storming entrance and taking a few minutes to get settled, he offered his apology and explained he had gone to the wrong prison.

Within the short time it took for the DA representative to get seated and sort himself out, it all changed. The commissioner put his jacket back on, and it felt as if the temperature in the room had dropped by 20 degrees. Then the panel asked the DA representative if he wanted to make a statement. As soon as he used the name I had previously been under (John Wetmore), my attorney reminded him I was only to be referred to as Morgan James Kane. The panel explained my name had not been changed, only corrected to what it should have been in 1984.

With a look like he had been scolded, he turned to me and said, 'Morgan James Kane, that's a pretty cool name, so how did you come by that?' To which I answered, 'My mum gave it to me!' He appeared completely shocked by my answer, as well as the fact I had dared to look him in the eyes and speak to him. Inmates could only address the DA representative by way of the appointed attorney, never directly. He immediately threw out the fact that the US government had taken my military service record away, as I had served under the name of John Raymond Wetmore, the name given to me by the man who purchased me when I was 14, and that I now had a deportation order levied against me. He said he didn't believe I was English because I didn't sound like Dick Van Dyke from *Mary Poppins*, which is the worst Cockney accent ever, or even Sean Connery, who just happens to be Scottish. The commissioner did have the sense to tell him that as I had been living in the US since before I could talk, it wasn't unreasonable not to have an English accent.

The panel then asked him why he might oppose me being found suitable for parole, given that if released

I would most certainly be taken into custody and processed for deportation. He responded that since the US government was saying I had never served in the military, how could anyone be certain what I was doing during those four years. Quite possibly, I had been committing crimes.

My next move was not my best or brightest. As neither of the panel members or my attorney chose to speak against such nonsense, I felt I needed to correct the record. My life was on the line here, and I couldn't let this ignorant idiot muddy the water. I stood up, looked at him and said, 'Hey stupid, they didn't say I wasn't in the military, they just said because I had served under an identity that wasn't mine, they weren't going to give me credit for it'. I knew the moment the words left my mouth that I wouldn't be found suitable, and I wouldn't be going home anytime soon. For some reason I wanted to believe that the panel members, my attorney and even the guard in the room had to be thinking exactly what I had said, and so I hoped it might not be as costly as it ultimately was.

After a few moments of silence, the commissioner stated he thought I had a work ethic to be proud of, and that most of my efforts in prison seemed to be focused on being able to get and keep employment once I was released. He felt I needed to continue on to achieving a 'better balance' and that though I had taken a number of self-help programmes, after witnessing my outburst he believed that I should focus on anger management courses (which I had already taken and were listed in the record). The psychologist's evaluation had actually stated 'low risk if released' and added, 'he did not think I needed more therapy, but that I should be allowed to be deported home and I would adjust well'. They deliberated for less than five minutes before giving me a five-year denial under new legislation which had lengthened all parole denials.

Chapter 22

SUITABLE FOR RELEASE

2013 – After dealing with the shock of my last hearing, I was feeling a bit gun-shy about my sixth. Since the Victim's Bill of Rights had come in, the majority of people I knew going to board hearings had been receiving not only longer denials, but even more substantial ones. At least a dozen guys who had always received three-year denials because of minor rule violations, were now instead getting seven or 10-year denials. That was suddenly a whole decade being taken from a man. The emotional toll that it took was devastating, and there were a few who couldn't handle the reality of it and chose to end their lives. Trying to be positive and look for the light at the end of the tunnel was becoming harder every day.

I went into this hearing with some trepidation, even

though I knew I had done all I had been asked by previous parole board panels and actually much more. I still realised it would always come down to the individuals sitting on the other side of the table who would more than likely make a 'personal feeling' decision and not one necessarily based on the facts of the case or all that I had accomplished while incarcerated.

Even though I was assigned a state-appointed attorney, this time I got a private one who was well respected by a lot of inmates. He wasn't there just for the money, but had a sense of justice and did not like to see it perverted by those who had the power. He had been instrumental in helping a number of guys get found suitable, and many more win their appeals in the court. Here was a man with real integrity and true professionalism. He also came to see me three times before my hearing, so we could work out the best way for me to present myself to the panel. He said not to worry about the DA representative, that was his job.

At the hearing, everyone was there on time and my attorney had shown up almost an hour before to give me a good old pep talk. I will give him this, he didn't like to lose and he acted as if he had as much at stake as I did – though that wasn't true, because I was fighting for my life and he was fighting for his reputation. Every time an attorney is present when an inmate is found suitable, it goes on their record. Every win ultimately gains more clients, and thus more revenue for the attorney.

With this hearing, I got a completely different panel with a male commissioner and a female deputy commissioner. They presented themselves as the most professional panel I ever sat before. Immediately before the start of the hearing, the deputy commissioner cautioned the DA representative about trying to evoke emotional outbursts from me or to present any information that had no relevance, which included 'historical' reports, statements or conjectures. By the look on the DA rep's face, you could tell this didn't sit well with him. To add insult to injury, she ended her admonishment by saying if he failed to follow her instructions, she would have him removed from the hearing.

From then on, the hearing went quite smoothly, with each panel member focusing on a different part of the file. They would read out a bit, then ask me some questions. You got the feeling that they were interested in my answers, and even asked me to take my time as they wanted me to be relaxed when speaking. That in itself was a totally different experience. The commissioner even stopped the hearing to allow for a restroom and water break, again something I had never heard of happening. The commissioner was very interested to have me explain what I knew of my early childhood and where I was born. As this was a subject that I was not only interested in, but set my path for where I wanted to return, I started to go into the explanation that I thought he was asking for. My attorney nudged my knee, asked the panel to speak to me, and then said for me to keep my answer short so as not to bore the panel. I found myself cutting my sentence off midstream and sat back to await the next question.

The commissioner then said very directly, 'I have read everything about you that the Immigration and Custom Enforcement agency has put in your C-File, and I have to say it was quite something to read and like nothing I have ever come across.' This was the moment when the DA representative decided he had to interrupt by saying that he felt it needed to be put on record that I was nothing more than a common criminal, and that his office was strongly urging this panel to not find me suitable. The deputy commissioner again admonished the DA representative for getting ahead of himself, and he was warned to avoid another interruption.

The panel was impressed that I had not one but three psychological evaluations, including one from a private psychologist hired by those who paid for my attorney. All gave me a 'low risk assessment' and agreed that I had developed skills that would aid me in finding employment upon release. The only point they didn't have in common was that the board psychologist thought that, 'being deported would cause me to have a chance of recidivism'. He hadn't seemed to grasp that it wasn't a choice that I had, but one made for me by the US government.

The other two psychologists said they thought, 'returning to the country of my birth would be a positive thing and they believed I would actually thrive once the initial culture shock was faced'. They agreed I already had in place a strong support network to aid my reintegration. That last part was extremely important, as the state of California only provides $200 'gate money' for someone to start their life over with, regardless how many years they have served. So, to have three evaluations with such positive comments seemed to impress the panel, even if the DA representative made faces when they were read into the record.

The hearing continued for another hour with the deputy commissioner putting on record all the courses, programmes and achievements I had accomplished in prison, as well as every support chrono I had received from a staff member. Now, the panel asked me why I thought I should be released. I told them that I understood the gravity of the loss of someone's life and how it doesn't just affect the person who lost their life, but every family member and friend they had. But beyond that it impacts all of society and that anytime someone does something which causes their community to be harmed, it harms the essence of what it means to be a civilised person.

The part I played was just as serious as if I had actually taken the victim's life, and so the fact that I was sent to prison was a proper outcome and though I could not undo anything that resulted in the loss of life, I had tried to help prevent other guys I met in prison from continuing with their lifestyle until they found themselves exactly where I was today. I had been doing all I could over the last 30 years to try to be better, be more caring and especially to be more conscious of how my actions, regardless how small, could have a devastating effect on others. Now I seriously think before I made decisions, something I could honestly say had not been a part of my previous behaviour. It was my plan that if found suitable, and I know I would be deported back to the UK, that I would continue to work to be a better person in the future and a contributing member of society.

It was then my attorney's time to speak, and to say that I had the surprise of my life would be an understatement. He began by saying that anyone who had a sense of decency when reading my life history would see that by just the slightest intervention early on in my life, none of us would be here today. He posed the question to the panel how was it possible for a child to be brought into the United States by someone not related to the child, if not illegally, and then move that same child through one state after another across the country while no one noticed or, if they did notice, didn't care. Why was I never sent to a public school until after I had been sold to an American couple, who for some reason 'needed' to replace a boy they had adopted. Surely others had to know of the plight of both these boys, yet again no one felt it was worth reporting. He went on to tell them, 'Here before you sits a man whose whole life from the very beginning was stolen from him, first by his paternal grandmother and apparently uncaring parents, then by the woman entrusted to take him to Canada, only to steal him and smuggle him into America, and used the ruse for nearly 12 years she was his mother, never telling him the truth. Then, when she could no longer care for him, sold him off for her financial benefit to a family who couldn't even seem able to care for the children they had adopted. This family did not lavish the child with love and affection, rather they abused him physically and emotionally, for their own pleasure.'

My attorney went on to tell the board that, after serving in the US Navy during the very trying times of the Vietnam era as a corpsman with the US Marines, 'he was yet again abandoned by the very country he served, as were so many other veterans of that conflict.' He added that many vets who were struggling with PTSD, which I had been diagnosed with, found themselves in dire straits; some become homelesss, drug addicts, commit suicide and a good number make wrong and completely irrational choices that land them in prison. He urged them to 'find it in your power, if not your hearts, to grant a second chance.'

He continued by saying that I would be 'sent away back to a country that didn't keep him safe initially and who may not welcome him back' and that it would be 'more humane to send him much sooner than later, as we all know adapting to life after prison can be hard, but imagine having to do this in a different country and with no family or friends.'

He highlighted that I was 'one of those rare individuals who struggled against peer pressure and prison politics, not only rising above it, but he was often involved in trying to help other, often younger inmates, find more positive things to do with their time.' My attorney also pointed out that supervisors at different prisons 'seem to express the same sentiment of how he carried himself even through adversity to be someone who could be trusted, who showed integrity and above all showed kindness and respect to all, be they staff or inmates.'

He held nothing back in support of me. He went on to

say, 'If this is not a prime example of the kind of man that society should want out in the world, well then, in my opinion, the human race as a whole is doomed, because every day, the prison system lets back out to the streets active gang members, drug dealers and users, those that prey on the elderly, women and our children.'

And he was not finished there, with his closing comments to the panel being, 'Here you have a chance to make a positive statement with Mr Kane, show him all his efforts have not been in vain, and if given the opportunity, I am sure without a doubt, he will carry on doing the right thing and helping those in need. This will be a decision you can live with, better yet, it will be a decision that will let you sleep at night.'

With that final statement, my attorney sat down without even looking at me. What a performance! The first time anyone had ever spoken up for me in such a fashion. Not that it was entirely true, of course. I was never homeless and, on the streets, or a drug addict. When I was arrested, I had bought my own house and had my own business, employing several staff.

You could see that the panel had heard every word. I wasn't sure whether it would resonate with them, but was something they would speak about long after the hearing, regardless of the outcome. The DA representative looked completely confused, like he was trying to shake off having been hit with a cricket bat. After five minutes of the panel whispering between themselves, the commissioner asked the DA representative if he would like to make his closing statement.

When he rose to his feet, he was still shuffling through his papers. He kept looking first at me and then the panel. Then he started off with the fact Fresno County was in opposition to inmate Kane being found suitable as it was their opinion that he 'was still an unreasonable risk to society if released'. He paused and took a look around to see what kind of reaction he may have evoked. It seemed that everyone was waiting to hear the rest of what he might have to say. He then launched his attack, 'I have listened to the convicted and to his attorney speak about how he has changed, even matured some might think, but really we all know that once someone has committed a crime, they are set upon a path that will keep bringing them back to prison, after committing more offences and creating a swath of victims in their wake. You cannot rehabilitate any of them. We tell the public that we have provided these so-called self-help courses and even Alcoholics Anonymous programmes, yet let's not fool ourselves into believing any of that works. Ask yourselves how many inmates have come before you with AA chronos for attendance and, at the same time, disciplinary chronos for using drugs and alcohol.'

He then stopped to take another look at the panel to try to get a sign he was getting through to them.

He paused for so long it caused the commissioner to ask if he was done with his statement. The DA representative responded, 'No, I was just gathering my thoughts'. So, the commissioner told him to continue but to be brief as they would like to deliberate before lunch. He conceding 'that inmate Kane had never been found in possession of drugs or alcohol in prison, and he could not find anything in any investigation reports showing he had used them before being incarcerated.'

He did feel that as I rode motorcycles, that surely would put me around criminal elements. He also noted that it had been more than two decades since I had received a disciplinary write-up even of the most minor kind, but could it be I had become much better at concealing criminal activity, which would make me all the more dangerous. In conclusion, he said he must strongly object to any chance that I might be found suitable and would take it personally if the panel did not do as Fresno County insisted. Giving me and my attorney a smug smile, he sat down feeling, I am sure, as if he had thrown dirt in my face.

My attorney had told me a number of times that no matter what the DA representative said, I was not to react. He told me not to even look at the guy, rather give my full attention to the parole panel and don't let them see that what was being said had fazed me. I knew this would be hard, but as this attorney was actually putting in the time to try to help me, the very least I could do was maintain my composure, when I really would like to face down the man who was speaking negatively about me.

The commissioner announced that the hearing would be recessed, so the panel could deliberate. With that, my attorney and I were led out of the hearing room and into a holding area. I asked my attorney how he thought it went, and he said there had been a good feeling, especially because of the closing statement the DA representative had given. He told me to relax, as he expected it would take at least 30 minutes.

Less than ten minutes later, the guard came and said the panel was back and ready to resume. My attorney looked at me and said he was sorry, because short deliberations almost always meant a denial. But he told me not to show any emotion or even stare in the direction of the panel when the decision was read, as anything I do will be used against me at my next hearing.

As we walked into the room, I could see a smirk on the face of the DA representative. Taking our seats, the commissioner started by telling me that I was one of the most unusual cases he had ever read through and that, quite frankly, if it had not been documented so completely by reliable sources of two different governments, he would have thought that it was something from the mind of a Hollywood screenwriter. He actually turned to the deputy commissioner to ask if she agreed, and she commented that it wouldn't surprise her if one day my life story became a film.

The commissioner started up again by saying that he felt my whole life read like a Victorian novel, and asked if I had ever thought about writing a book. To which I responded, 'No.' He said that if I got out of prison, I should pursue the idea and have it published. He then said something I thought was strange, as he added, 'I will be terribly disappointed in you if you do not try and get your story out to the masses.' Now that I have written something of my life story, I have to wonder if he has ever read it.

He said that he thought I had accomplished a great deal in prison which would serve me well once released, and he could tell by all the laudatory chronos from staff that they felt I deserved a second chance. He said he did wonder what kind of life I would have as I would be deported to the United Kingdom, and if the strain might cause me to fail. He hoped there may be some safeguards in place to prevent me from ever becoming involved in any activities that could bring me back into prison. He felt given just the slightest chance to be successful, I would take full advantage and make the most of every opportunity.

The commissioner continued, saying a good motorcycle mechanic was worth his weight in gold. He mentioned that I had developed woodworking and carving skills along with having learned to draw, and that he was amazed I had been displayed in the Royal Festival Hall in London and the piece had sold. All these were the definite positives. However, he said he would be amiss if he did not lay out the negatives. They had read through the transcripts of the five previous hearings and how each of those panels had reached their decisions to deny my release. He believed that, at times, there were points that previous panels may have either overlooked or not recognised the significance of.

After taking a pause which felt like minutes, but was only a few seconds, he said the biggest flaw I had was that I cared far more for others than I did for myself, and as a child I had been the one who took care of the woman I believed was my mother when she had been beaten up or had too much drink. In the US Navy, I had trained to be a Hospital Corpsman, and volunteered to be attached to the Marines. He asked if I realised that meant if I found myself in a combat situation, it would be expected to run towards gunfire to rescue and care for a wounded marine. I told him yes, and that I had done what was necessary to protect my men. He then asked, 'Why would you take such risks with your life?' I responded, 'It was my duty to get them home to their families and I felt personally responsible for each man under my care.'

It was at this point he said, 'And when you came home and found a man dead on your living room floor, you again stepped up to try to protect others – yet you didn't know what part in the man's death your wife may have played. Then, when it looked as if she would likely be found guilty and sent to death row, you accepted an offer to save her. Why is that?'

I took a moment and then said, 'I felt somehow responsible that whatever was going on, I knew she could not survive prison, even if she was not put to death and, of course, my son needed his mother'. The commissioner gave me a look that seemed to convey some concern, and then said, 'Don't you think he needed his father?' I told him, 'Quite honestly I don't know how to be a father; I never had one and outside my gunny sergeant, I never had a strong male figure in my life. But I have known a lot of strong women who helped raise me and so I wanted him to have what I hoped was the best chance at a good life. What would he think if, years later, he found out I had the chance to save his mother and didn't? I would rather he forgot me than hate me.'

For a moment there seemed to be some emotion in the eyes of the deputy commissioner, though she restrained herself from saying anything. After mulling over my answer, the commissioner said, 'You have just confirmed what I saw in everything about you in every report, psychological evaluation and staff chrono. You have little concern for your own self, yet you seem to value the lives of others, even those you don't know. This is something you need to work on, and I don't mean stop caring for others, but just realise you are important as well. Don't short change yourself and know that everyone whose life you touched in some positive way will not only likely remember it, but at some point, tell others about you. So, you have made a difference and if nothing else today, you can at least take that bit with you from this hearing.'

I looked at my attorney, and I could see by the look on his face that he felt I had done a good job with my answers to the commissioner's questions. Now was the moment we had been waiting for... the reading of the decision. The deputy commissioner straightened herself up in her chair, then picking up the one sheet of paper in front of her, she looked me straight in the eye as she began to read, 'Mr. Kane, after nearly three hours and careful review of all the evidence, reports, evaluations and comments placed before this panel, the commissioner and I would like to say that we find you suitable for release.'

Wait a moment! My mind stopped, and I could feel the gears grinding as it tried to process what was just said. I remember looking over to my attorney, and he was smiling. Then a quick look at the DA representative and he was just stuffing his papers back into his briefcase. It was like I had gone deaf, as I heard no sound. Did she say 'found suitable'? My mind was still trying to collect that thought. When I looked back at her, she was smiling and the commissioner was smiling while stretching his hand towards me. She could see I was looking confused, and so she said it again, 'Yes, Mr. Kane, this panel finds you suitable.' I quickly shook the commissioner's hand and then her hand that appeared from nowhere, and thanked them so much.

The commissioner went on to say that the decision would still have to go before the full parole board, and they would have up to four months in which to make a decision to let it stand, modify it or deny it. If it gets passed, then it goes to the governors' office where a decision would be made in 30 days as to whether they would approve it, refuse to review it (either of those would result in my going home) or deny it and I would be given another date to return to a parole board hearing for another try. He explained that in the panel's decision, they were trying to answer any concern that might be raised and prevent any reason as to why I should not be released. With that, the panel wished me luck on a new life and new start in Britain, and the commissioner restated about how he would be disappointed if I didn't write a book.

The guard escorted my attorney and I back to the holding area and gave me the decision sheet. He told me, 'Congratulations Kane, you deserve it.' We sat in that room for about 15 minutes discussing the hearing, and my attorney said he was happy for me, though he had been concerned that I was going to be denied. Short deliberations usually mean that the panel has made up their minds before they even start the hearing. He was also amazed at how open the commissioner was when speaking to me about what he had read, and that he not only encouraged me, but basically insisted that I had to write a book about my life.

The guard let my attorney out and returned a few minutes later to release me from the hearing area so I could go back to my housing unit to begin to process the reality that I had been found 'suitable'. No one can explain just how it feels to hear that word 'suitable' at the parole board. Some guys come back in tears, making others think they had been given a long denial, only to be surprised that they had been found 'suitable'.

Chapter 23

DENIED – 'BECAUSE I CAN'

We all know the board's decision can be changed at any time during the 150-day wait for the decision to be finalised, and there are plenty of guys that happens to. I knew a couple of guys who had it happen to them more than once, which is devastating. I have even seen it break a person. So, it has to be taken with cautious satisfaction.

Of course, it was amazing to walk down the long hallway back to my cell and have staff congratulate me. As I passed the library, the windows were filled with faces, some I knew, though most I didn't, yet all cheering me on and giving me the thumbs up. By the time I finally reached my cell, I was totally knackered and just wanted to lay down and sleep. As I put down my packet of paperwork, I had taken to the hearing,

I could hear my cellmate telling others I had been found suitable and not to bother me until later. It was expected for people to ask about the hearing – who was on the panel, what attorney did you have, what kinds of questions did they ask?

Unfortunately, it did not end happily for me. Instead of being sent back to the UK in 2013, I remained in prison, in California, because Governor Jerry Brown, took my date.

Just two days before I was to get out, I received notice from his office that he was denying my parole. The worst bit for me was the reason he gave for reversing the board's decision. His reason was, 'Because I can.' How can a person beat something like that? There was no legal reason, nothing tangible I could point to and say he was wrong when submitting a writ into the courts, which have previously ruled that a board panel member or the governor's personal feeling was an acceptable reason for denying parole. The only saving grace was that there was an automatic re-hearing in one year on a governor's denial.

2014 – I was about to go into my seventh parole hearing after being found 'suitable' 12 months previously. Nothing had changed, except I had another year of positive programming, one more year of laudatory chronos to present and more of a determination I was going to get my date back from the parole board panel. I could not see why I wouldn't be given back my date.

Most people say if there was ever a time to hire a private attorney, then this was it. Having been found suitable, it should make it easier for a private attorney to build on the previous win. I could not afford to hire a private attorney; it was done through the efforts of others on the outside. The one I got was in the top ten, so for the money paid and the services we got, I can't complain and at the time felt he did have my best interests at heart. He had come highly recommended.

He had been quite interested in knowing who was on my previous board panel. When I told him, he said that was one of the best to get and, with luck, we might get one or both members again, which would only work in our favour, especially since I had been programming positively. Often when someone got their date taken by the governor, they would get upset and do something stupid, catching a disciplinary write-up which would then be used negatively against them at the next parole board hearing.

He was surprised when I told him of the commissioner's interest in my life and his encouragement to write a book. I told him how the DA representative wasn't quite as impressed with me or the statements made by the panel. He told me that we would just deal with the DA if needed, otherwise we will just ignore them, focusing primarily on the panel and presenting ourselves the best way we could. He even told me to press my clothes before the hearing as he wanted them to see me as someone who takes that extra bit to prepare. My attorney even gave me a special folder for all the papers I wanted to bring.

We would practise going over questions he thought the panel might ask. He wanted me to be prepared for everything that might be thrown at us. An observer from a parole board watch group called Lifer Support Alliance (LSA) had been granted permission by CDC head office in Sacramento to sit in and watch (though they were not allowed to speak or participate). My attorney thought the panel members would be careful not to do or say anything, when getting documented. If I needed to file a writ with the court, not only would I have my hearing transcript, but there would be an independent report of what happened as well. I didn't see a downside to them being there.

A couple of days before the hearing, I got out my best set of 'blues' (denim jeans and blue button-down shirt – I had held onto them for more than 15 years just for special occasions – board hearings or visits). I washed and ironed them so that they looked sharp, and hoped it may give me that extra bit to impress the panel, as my attorney had said. As I was going with a paid attorney, I was expecting that he would do a much more engaging defence for me than if he was just appointed. To this point, he had not disappointed me and as I arrived at the hearing area, my attorney had shown up more than 45 minutes early to continue to work on what he called his 'game plan' for the day.

He seemed to be in an upbeat mood and said he had every confidence that we would prevail. He was happy with the fact we would have a woman and a man, and though he did not know the man, he did know the woman who was the commissioner and had found her reasonable to deal with. This, of course, made me feel all the better. He explained that he had appeared before this particular commissioner on a few dozen occasions and said that, with a few rare exceptions, she would generally go with the recommendation of the psychological evaluations. For me, this was good news as I had nothing but being a 'low risk' for the last eight FAD evaluations. The last four had even included comments like 'Well adjusted', 'Not institutionalised', 'Will likely do well in a free society', and my favourite, 'Should be able to adjust with being deported to the UK with little adjustment time needed'. It would seem that this hearing should be a short one and hopefully provide me with the outcome I wanted – to go back for round two with the governor.

As the hearing started, everything seemed to be heading to a very positive result. The deputy commissioner kept giving me nervous corners of the mouth smiles. I had found out that this was only his third or fourth hearing, so I assumed that was why he felt uncomfortable. The commissioner was very much in control, and although she showed her forcefulness at times, she otherwise seemed to allow each person in turn to speak up. The DA representative was one who I had once previously, and though he was here to do his job, which was to keep me in prison, by no means did he go out of his way to try to make me look worse than the record reflected, and for that I was appreciative.

It was about midway through that I got this funny feeling that something wasn't quite right with the commissioner when she was suddenly in the middle of a sentence, stopped abruptly and said, 'I am confused, who are we doing this hearing for – inmate Kane or an inmate Wetmore, and which one is British and are we sure the other is an American? Why is there a deportation notice in the file?' The fact that these things should come up now really caused concern, even on the deputy commissioner's face, and he immediately suggested that the hearing be stopped for a short break.

After being escorted to a room where my attorney and I could talk, it seemed that the commissioner was having a problem. We discussed if it was possibly a medical one or just a cognitive one, but I did express my concern. My attorney was doing his best to reassure me. Still, there was this feeling of dread I couldn't shake. It was almost an hour before we were called back into the hearing room, and you could see that the DA representative was even showing signs that he had no idea what was going on.

We sat waiting for one of the panel members to say something, and even that took a few more minutes. The commissioner said we were back on the record and that she couldn't make heads or tails of my C-File. It was as clear as day that in no way had she done any preparation for my hearing.

Then she said rather pointedly that she preferred hearings where things are laid out in a very straightforward manner and do not deviate, which for her was quite confusing. She started to ramble on about how she couldn't understand how any of my psychological evaluations could accurately predict my future behaviour, and made some comment about not even knowing what she would feel like eating for lunch.

My attorney tried to interject something, and got as far as saying 'Lady commissioner', when she cut him off by saying, 'How do you know I am a lady? Do you feel that makes me less qualified than the gentleman deputy commissioner to my left?' The look she gave my attorney said the rest, which could be interpreted to mean 'shut up'.

The hearing was into its third hour when just as abruptly she announced that the panel would now adjourn for their deliberations. Now it was the DA representative who spoke up, citing he had not been allowed to make a statement. The commissioner gave him a hard stare and then said, 'Well let me see if we have it correct, the Fresno County district attorney's office vigorously opposes any finding of suitability in the case of inmate Kane and if this panel was to find him suitable, they would then fight it to their highest ability to whichever authority they believed would reverse this panel's decision. Does that sum up what you were going to say?' The DA rep just nodded his head in agreement, which prompted the retort, 'You will have to voice your answer, as nods are not registered on the tape'. He said, 'Yes, that would seem to meet the basis of what my argument would have been, thank you.'

The commissioner turned to my attorney and told him, 'I don't feel this panel needs to hear from you either, as I can rest assured you will be touting all the fine qualities and personal strides your client has made.

As well as wanting to remind us of all of his accomplishments with vocational training and work experiences, and the fact he has many laudatory chronos from staff who attest to him being a fine individual. Have I got that right?' My attorney said, 'You are correct, though I would also remind the panel that he will be deported and, therefore, not be the responsibility of the people of the state of California should he choose to fail to adjust on the outside.'

We all had no idea what was going through her mind as we all exited the hearing room. The guard waited with us to say that he was constantly surprised at the way some panels acted, and that this one was for the books.

My attorney said that he was completely surprised at her behaviour and that he had never known her to act this way. For me it was knowing, whatever the cause, it was my life that would be affected, and I could only hope in a good way. The times while you wait to be called back in to hear what they have decided were by far the hardest part of the whole ordeal. Some people will take a denial badly, throwing paperwork, and in some extreme cases even launching themselves over the table at the panel members, which never works out well for the inmate. Some will break down crying no matter if they get denied or found suitable. I tended to stay very stoic, especially when I had been found suitable, though that may have been shock, having finally made it. From the beginning, doing time had not been easy, not that I couldn't do it, just that every time I turned around there seemed to be someone trying to put bumps in my way. Some people tried to say I was paranoid, that I might think people were out to get me, but I would explain that I 'knew' people had been out to get me all my life and had documents to prove it, so what I had was actually 'heightened awareness'.

We were called back into the hearing room for their decision, and it was going to be short, I could tell, as the two panel members had already put aside my file and I could see the name of the next guy they would be seeing on the file in front of them. The commissioner said that as they had two more individuals to hear, she would get right to it. 'We have decided that you have programmed in a limited manner over your years of incarceration and it is the opinion of this panel that you do not meet the standard needed to be found suitable, therefore we find you unsuitable for parole'. She paused for a moment and looked at me, most certainly trying to gauge my response, of which I gave none. She continued, 'We feel to give you the time and incentive to avail yourself to the opportunities around you, we are giving you a five-year denial and wish you well. It is also recommended that you do something about getting your file cleaned up so that it is easier for the next panel to understand.'

I was taken to the hold cell, where my attorney spoke to me about getting my appeal filed within weeks. He was sure that a court would recognise that this hearing was a fiasco. I, of course, knew that I would just have to keep plugging away and not do anything to give the next panel extra reasons to deny me, though the ones used by this one were completely wrong. I had done so much more programming than many who had already gone home. This was my fight to win or lose, and I chose to push onward and upward.

My attorney did get my writ filed and though it took time going through three courts, we finally got a ruling that would bring me back to the parole board in two years instead of five. In the end, it was this seventh hearing that held the key which unlocked my future. During the course of the hearing, somehow my attorney had managed to pick up a couple of documents from the district attorney, one of which I had never seen before and one which I had lost years ago. At the time it was given to me, I would not have understood the signifi-cance. The second document was called my change of plea hearing, a transcript of the hearing back in 1984, when I pleaded guilty to save my wife from execution.

I had tried to obtain a copy a few years before, but the court told me that their records were only kept for 20 years and so it had been destroyed. On reading it again, I could see how coerced I was into taking the plea, even to the point where proceedings were adjourned for the district attorney to tell my attorney what I had to say. But far more important, and shocking, to me, I saw that the trial judge, right near the start of the proceedings, read out to me the format of words that is used in a trial for every illegal alien. I could not believe it! Yes, back in 1984, everyone in that courtroom, apart from myself that is, knew that I had not been adopted, knew that my name was not legally John Wetmore, the name I was charged under, had not told me what they knew, and more importantly, had not told immigration about my status. It follows, that as they knew I was using the social security number that had been allocated to a child called John Wetmore, his disappearance should have been investigated, and it obviously wasn't. No wonder the Fresno DA's office wanted to keep me in custody. Whatever was going on back in 1984, my guess is that they didn't want it to come out.

Each parole panel is supposed to read the paperwork on you prior to your hearing, including the Probation Officer's Report (POR). This document is written by a probation officer prior to you being sentenced.

Strangely, mine was written by a man who had known me since I was first brought to Fresno by Dr Wetmore, as they were friends. It was supposed to contain your history, so that the judge could decide on your sentence. I had my three-page battered copy, which said nothing about any previous crimes, hardly surprising as I hadn't committed any. The POR that my attorney got his hands on, and which every board had read prior to every hearing, was 11 pages long. The document I held was a 'cut and paste' job, of sections of the actual POR, done I might add, in 1984, which was before the days of cut and paste via a computer. Somebody went to a lot of trouble to make up the document that I held. And why do you think that was? Because we worked out that the board's 11-page POR held more than 20 provable lies about me, including a string of crimes for which I had supposedly been convicted, including one, believe it or not, when I was actually out of the US while serving with the US Marines. If I had committed half the crimes listed, I would never have got into the military in the first place, yet on all my boards up until 2006 when my service records were deleted, every board had no trouble accepting and accusing me of these crimes, as well as accepting that I had a four-year service record.

Chapter 24

NINE AND OUT

2016 – I couldn't believe it, but I found myself about to go into my eighth parole hearing. Nothing had changed, except I had two more years of positive programming, two more years of laudatory chronos and two more years of my life wasted. Because the attorney who had been hired to represent me at the last hearing had at least got me back early, the people who hired him believed he deserved another chance. He had even offered this hearing for a discount. They retained him and as I believed he was more concerned about his reputation than whether I met parole, I felt he would bring his 'A' game to prove that he was as good as he believed he was.

I followed the same instructions he had given me before my last hearing. I had my best set of blues ready to wear, and I had all my documents properly tagged and filed. As he had done previously, he came to see me a number of times to ensure I would be ready. He was always quite positive about our chances (well not ours, but mine as nothing could affect whether he went home after the hearing), leaving every one of our visits by saying, 'Don't worry, this time is it.'

When I arrived half an hour before the hearing, one of the guards ushered me into one of the holding tanks. I could see that in one of the interview rooms there was another inmate either with his attorney preparing for a hearing or being interviewed by a psychologist for an evaluation. After watching for a few moments, I could tell it was a psych interview, the inmate was sitting too rigidly, and you could see no friendliness that usually came with a discussion with an attorney, even a state appointed one.

My attorney showed up five minutes before we went into the hearing. He had been checking on who the panel would be. He did the old, 'Do you want the good news or the not so good news.' I asked for the 'not so good news'. We didn't have any of my last panel, but he had never seen the new panel before and so didn't know how they were going to be. The good news was the LSA had sent two people to observe the hearing. He assured me that this would be a factor in the panel acting properly, and he felt it increased our chances of me being found suitable again.

I recognised the DA representative from my hearing

in 2009 and I whispered to my attorney, who had faced the guy before. I got smiles from the two LSA observers, who were poised with pads and pens.

This panel consisted of two women, who were both dressed smartly and, it seemed, were the image of true professionals. My attorney was given the opportunity to speak first. He gave a rousing speech about all my accomplishments and how the previous panel had applauded them. He believed that I was ready to re-join society and be a productive member, and reminded them that I was to be deported to the UK.

Once my attorney sat down, it was the DA representative's time to speak. He started with the same old rhetoric about how Fresno County opposed any possibility of me being found suitable again. They were against the federal government taking me into custody, should I be found suitable, and allowing me to be deported. His next statement would direct the rest of the hearing for the next two hours. He chose to point out in the last meeting, in front of the previous panel, I had attempted to make him look like a fool when he was trying to inform them that the US government had taken away my military service record. Though he did admit that he may have been a little overzealous in his misinterpretation of what that had actually meant, he believed that the fact that I had served under an identity not of my own should certainly cause this panel to find me unsuitable.

He was about to continue with his spiel when the commissioner told him to sit down, that was enough. She did it with such a tone and volume, you had to wonder if the rest of the prison heard her. She stood up and leaned on the table, looked around the room and finally fixed her eyes on me. Then, in what started as a deep growl rising to a scream, she said, 'I know all about Vietnam era veterans and their PTSD, I was married to one! You are all pieces of shit and should be treated like rabid dogs. Oh sure, you can put on a nice face and for a while act like you're civilised, but we both know there is a monster inside waiting to rip out and destroy lives.' I took a moment to take a quick look at everyone else's faces in the room, and shock doesn't even begin to describe what I saw.

The next two hours continued with her putting on record how horribly her ex-husband treated her and their children, and how the statistics show that every veteran was a ticking time bomb. She felt let down by the US government who, after teaching us the skills we needed to go to war, would just let us loose on the unsuspecting public to contend with our outbursts and violence. Even the deputy commissioner didn't try to interrupt as she continued ranting and raving at me about how miserable her husband had been. She went into his drinking, drug use and lying to her, points that when my attorney tried to tell her did not apply to me, got him reprimanded and told him to 'shut up!'

I kept thinking the guard in the room was going to grab me and take me out of the room, as he must have been concerned I might get mad and display the behaviour she was putting on all veterans. I knew the guard was a veteran, and this couldn't have been comfortable for him to sit through. The commissioner made some negative comments about all the psychologists who had evaluated me over the last 15 years, and that they all gave me 'low risk' assessments. She preferred to use the one that had been done in my second year. It was about 30 years old, but she thought it was valid as it was the worst I had ever had, and listed me as a 'moderate to low risk.'

My only hope was that the two LSA observers were getting every word, though I doubted it as the commissioner was in such a rage some words weren't even making it past her lips. I wasn't sure if it would ever end. I knew this hearing was so far gone that I would not get a suitable decision, or even a split decision.

It stopped just as quickly as it had started. The commissioner looked about the room and said, 'We will now deliberate and make a decision.' With that, the guard came and got me and walked me into a holding cell. My attorney had been pulled to the side by the DA representative, while the two LSA observers were shown to another room. The guard brought me a glass of water and said, 'Kane, I have never experienced anything like that in my 10 years as a board hearing officer. That was pretty rough, and I want you to know I really appreciate the fact you held it together. Not sure if I could have if she had been speaking to me like that, and I will be documenting this in the log and speaking to the sergeant when I can.' As he left, he paused for a moment to ask if I needed anything else.

My attorney walked in and I could see he was still shaken by the whole thing. Looking at me, he said, 'The DA rep says he is going to report this to his boss in Fresno County. He is not so unhappy that you are likely to be denied, but the fact he didn't get to put on his performance to say what a terrible person you are. Though he did agree with me that he had never sat in on a hearing that was as venomous from a panel member before. There is little chance this decision will go in your favour, so I want you to sit there and don't say or do anything that might make it worse. I will do your writ to the courts Pro Bono, because I feel you got a raw deal and should have been found suitable again.'

About half an hour later, we were all called back. It

was a calmer conversation, and the deputy commissioner finally got to say a few things about the fact that
the panel applauded my accomplishments but felt there
were shortcomings that I needed to work on for my next
hearing. It was then the commissioner said with a bit of
glee in her eyes, while looking directly at me, 'Inmate
Kane, you are found to be an unreasonable risk to
society, should you be released on parole and based on
that determination this panel finds you unsuitable. We
have also determined that you are given a three years
denial. This panel feels that you need to do some real
soul-searching into whether you have done all you can
to allow any future panel to feel comfortable with your
progress.'

Suddenly, my attorney jumps up and sprints from the
room. Everyone was shocked beyond words; this was
not the behaviour usually displayed by any attorney.
There were a few moments of silence, and then the
guard told me to stand up and exit the room. He took
me into one of the interview rooms and there was my
attorney, who apologised for his actions and said he was
just so aggravated that I didn't get a fair hearing.

He said that not only would he be doing my writ
for free, but that as he didn't feel he had a chance to
represent me, he didn't feel he had earned his pay for
doing the job, and so he would also represent me at my

next hearing for free as well. The two LSA observers stopped by to say they would be writing up a full report and I would get a copy of it, as well as a copy being presented the next time they had a meeting with the secretary of the department of corrections & rehabilitation. They were amazed by the unprofessional behaviour of the commissioner. My attorney said he would be notifying other attorneys to be aware of this particular commissioner's outburst and if they found there had been a similar one, it was possible they might get her removed from panels.

But then something strange happened. Instead of honouring his promise, my attorney stopped answering my letters and refused my calls. As he did not keep his word on my appeal, I had to get another inmate in the law library to do it. It was granted, giving me a rehearing set for one year. The observers from LSA never sent me a copy of their report, which I found very disappointing, as I believed it would help me be found suitable at my next hearing. Some time later I did hear, through the grapevine, that both my attorney and LSA had been warned that if they continued to help me, they might find their other aims were difficult to achieve.

2017 – Ever since that last fiasco, I had tried to find out what happened to the attorney who represented me.

He had been paid almost $6,000 dollars. When I tried to call his office, my calls were not accepted, none of my letters were answered and even those who had hired him could not get him to respond.

They offered to hire me another attorney. However, I declined, not wanting them to throw away more money. Most disappointing was the fact that LSA, who had been so supportive and seemed to understand my situation, dropped off the radar. So, when it came time to sign the notification documents with my counsellor, I asked for an appointed attorney, subconsciously hoping I would get the same one who had been there when I had been found suitable.

I kept preparing to be as ready as I could for the panel's questions and hoping that this time, I would get my date back and find myself on my way home. I finally got called to an attorney visit. He wasn't the one I wanted, and I would find out that he was someone that most of the guys he represented didn't like. Not because he wasn't very good. It was because he was Nigerian and because he had such a heavy accent that they couldn't understand him. I tried to explain that the way to resolve that was not to listen to him, but instead watch his lips, as the mouth generally makes the same shape for the same letter, regardless of the accent. I found when I did this technique, I had no problem communicating with him which set us both at ease, as I realised not being understood by his clients had to be frustrating to him as well.

He came prepared, having read the transcript of the previous hearing thoroughly and was appalled, not only at how the commissioner acted, but that neither the deputy commissioner or the guard had tried to stop the hearing. I told him it was one of those 'deer in the head-lights' scenarios and because it came on so quickly and with such intensity, I thought everyone was in a state of shock. He told me not to worry, he would certainly say something if that happened when he was someone's counsel. He believed that in a case of someone possibly regaining their freedom, it was of the utmost importance that the hearing be fair and well managed.

He came to see me three times before the hearing and each time he spent several hours going over every document, chrono, and report in my C-File. I was amazed at how good he was in comparison to the majority of attorneys, both state appointed and privately hired. I am not sure how long he had been in the United States or when he had gone to law school, but he felt everyone deserved a fair hearing and had a right to be heard. Unlike some attorneys, he would not promise that I would be found suitable, only that he would not allow me to be verbally abused by either member of the panel or the DA representative, and assured me that any improprieties would be reported.

The day of the hearing came, though unlike others where there may be three or four inmates going before the parole board, today it was just me. The reason for that, I was told, was because my appeal over the last hearing had been decided in a review by the governing body of the board. It was their decision that made my hearing come so fast, and I could only hope this would be an omen of good things to come.

As usual, I arrived a bit early so I could have some extra time with my attorney in case he had anything he wanted to remind me of. His main advice had been that I needed not to talk too much, listen to any questions asked, take a moment to answer them with the shortest number of words as possible. He said it was important not to bring up any subject that they had not asked about, so as not to assist them in finding a reason to deny me when there was no reason.

My attorney was waiting for me and I could see that there was something on his mind. In the interview room, he looked at me gravely and said in a very calm and clear voice, 'We have the same panel as last year.' That information hit me like a ton of bricks. 'No, you can't be serious,' I responded, 'Really, how does that happen?' He went on to try to assure me that it would be all right and not to let it get to me. I told him after the last hearing being so unfair and with the commissioner so out of control, my pen pal in the UK and I had agreed if it should happen, I just would not put myself through it again. I told him I didn't want to go through all that again, having her spit her hate-filled venom at me for another few hours. So, let's postpone this hearing on the grounds that I do not feel I will get a fair and non-prejudicial panel based on their previous actions.

He shocked me when he said he thought I should go ahead and that I should just trust that he will not let things get out of hand. I responded, 'There is no way that this panel is going to find me suitable just one year after basically telling me I was the spawn of Satan. They did everything but talk bad about my mother.' He listened to me while I expressed my concerns and let him know I might not be able to go through that kind of vicious attack without speaking up and defending myself. When I had finally stopped talking, he very calmly said, 'Mr. Kane, I have done a lot of hearings and I can tell you the panel is made up of just people, all with their own little character flaws. Sometimes they let things in their personal life get in the way of them being subjective. I have seen panels completely change from being adversarial to being proper and compliant.' Taking a moment to watch for any reaction, he continued, 'I think we need to go in there and stick to our game plan and make it just that much harder to deny you. Rest assured, if it looks like it may get out of hand, I will stop the hearing and request a postponement. What do you think of that?'

I was having a hard time believing that this would work out in a good way, but for some reason, the fact that he seemed so confident meant I finally gave in. I did let him know I wouldn't wait very long for him to speak up if it started to go as before.

When the commissioner saw me, she gave just the slightest evidence of a smile out of the corner of her mouth, which to me meant we were in for round two. Ding, Ding! After she had gone around the room and had everyone say their name into the record, the hearing began by her saying, 'Thank you Mr. Kane, it is so nice that you were able to join us today and let's get on with the hearing.'

I still had a feeling of foreboding, as if the Sword of Damocles was hanging over my head. Other people have often said that they believed that I may have been born without a sense of fear because throughout my entire life I have been willingly to do things that others would not dare to, almost always with the intention of helping someone else. But this time, the fear was definitely based on concern for my own fate. So, I steadied myself for whatever the commissioner was going to throw at me today.

There was no one more surprised than I when the hearing just started to flow along, with no hint of her even mentioning a single thing about military service, or veterans. They seemed to be following the format that all panels were supposed to. They started with my early life, never mentioned any 'past crimes', skipped over anything to do with military service and went right into the commitment offence. Then, ever so briefly, the deputy commissioner added in a bit of my in-prison behaviour, on which both commended me. Then the commissioner went further and said that I should be proud of myself for not falling for the traps set in prison that cause so many to fail.

I was sure I must be sitting in an episode of the *Twilight Zone*, because there was no way this person sitting before me and talking to me was the same one from last year. Her demeanour was so professional, and she even had the deputy commissioner read all my vocational and self-help reports into the record, all the while remarking how well I had prepared, how I had become able to go out into the society and make a new life for myself.

The commissioner turned to the DA representative and asked him if he had anything to add. Though just before he could answer, she suddenly added, 'Please make sure it is not anything that has been said by a representative from Fresno County in any past hearings or it will be stricken from the record and not given any consideration.' That hit the guy right between the eyes. I had this guy at two other hearings, and he was the type that liked to just throw things out there to give the panel concern they may have missed something. By doing that, he would often be able to sway the panel into saying 'not suitable', rather than take the chance they did miss something and let a dangerous person out.

Now, with such restrictions put on him, he said he only had one thing he would like to voice. Everyone was watching as he prepared to bring forth this revelation of information that he hoped would get him a win. Clearing his throat, and only taking a glance at me before slightly turning to face the board, he began, 'I believe it is very important that this panel takes into consideration the fact that at present, inmate Kane has a standing order from DHS/ICE that if released he is to be deported back to the UK. How many people in this room believe he is at all British, I mean he doesn't even have a British accent. We can find no living relatives for him in the UK and so the district attorney's office of Fresno County strongly feels that if he were to be sent back that he, in all likelihood, would have to live a criminal lifestyle to be able to survive where he has no family or friends for support.'

He said the only circumstances under which his office might even think of a finding of suitability was if the board panel made a stipulation that the federal government could not take custody of inmate Kane until he had successfully been discharged from parole by the Fresno County parole division. With that, he sat back and seemed quite satisfied with his performance, that I am sure he had to ad-lib on the spot.

I am sure he thought he had done his office proud, that is until the commissioner started to speak. 'You do realise that this panel nor any branch of the state of California authority, can make any demands against the federal government, and certainly not override a federal court order given to Homeland Security in the matter as to whether or not to deport Mr. Kane. Then to the matter of whether he is British or not, that has been decided by two governments, the United States and that of the United Kingdom, and they have concluded he was. So your county's request is a moot point that will not even be considered by this panel.' With that, she turned to my attorney to ask if he had any information or wished to make any statement.

He looked at the panel and then in a slow methodical manner started to stack up the papers he had spread out throughout the hearing, while responding, 'Yes ma'am, Lady Commissioner, I would very much like to make a statement.' He was speaking much slower than I knew he normally did, and I could tell he was trying to make sure he pronounced every word as clearly as possible so there would not be any possible misunderstanding. 'I don't feel I need to sit here and point out to the panel or anyone else in the room the many accomplishments that Mr. Kane has done over the last 30-plus years. Nor does it need to be said that he has been a model prisoner and that is well expressed in laudatory chronos written by a number of staff members who have either worked with him or supervised him and, interestingly enough, many stated that he was the first inmate they ever wrote one for. What I do think has been overlooked since the beginning, was that Mr. Kane was brought into this country illegally as a child and then actually sold as declared by the man who bought him, one Dr. Wetmore, who had written an affidavit to the facts of his involvement. Those facts have never really been discussed at any of the parole hearings. Then the mere fact that he has had an order for removal placed on him since 2009 and here it is 2017, eight years later, and he is still waiting for that order to be enacted.'

He paused, looked at the DA representative, and then facing the panel again he continued, 'I find it amazing that the representative of the district attorney has not said that he or his office finds the trafficking of children abhorrent and vile in a civilised society. Yet he feels rather than allow Mr. Kane to be found suitable and returned to his native country, where at his age it will be hard to adjust for so many reasons, he would rather have him forced to stay here and parole to Fresno County for who knows how many years before allowing him to be sent home.'

I could see the DA representative's face was getting redder and the veins of his forehead were throbbing with every word coming from my attorney's mouth. Finally, my attorney said, 'I will conclude with, if Mr. Kane is not suitable now, I fear he will never be. There may soon come a day when he decides to stop being a performing animal for the amusement of others and realise that too much time has passed, he will decide to just stay in prison. If that is allowed to happen then this panel, its governing body and even society will have truly lost its way, for if you steal all hope, then you will see that others will stop attending these parole hearings, as they will be seen as a sham, and without any true substance. So, I ask that you find Mr. Kane suitable. It will be seen that there is still something to strive for. Let him be sent back to the UK and have a chance to rebuild his life if he can'. With that last statement, my attorney nodded, indicating he was finished.

All I could think was that either they were going to do

some real thinking on what he said, or it will have infuri-
ated them so much that I will get an even longer denial.
This whole hearing had been strange from the start, as
the commissioner was nothing like she had been at the
last one. It was almost as if she didn't remember me, and
so I had no idea of what would happen now. The commissioner thanked everyone for their participation, then
told the guard to escort me from the room and that we
would be called back once a decision had been made.

Back in the interview room, my attorney was surprised
when the guard wished me good luck, saying he thought
the hearing went well. I told my attorney that I really
liked his statement, though I am sure the DA representative did not, and that I didn't think he cared for how
the commissioner had spoken to him. He was honest
enough to say he had no idea about the decision, but
felt I had a better chance for a good outcome than if I
had chosen to postpone.

After almost 45 minutes of waiting, the guard came
to get us, saying that a decision had been made. Going
in, the DA representative was sitting there with a big
'cat who ate the canary' grin on his face, which did not
exactly fill me with confidence for a positive outcome.
Though now looking back, I realise it was his normal
look of an expected denial and nothing more. As soon
as the commissioner could see we were all back, seated

and focusing on her, she began by saying, 'We have weighed all the evidence that was presented before us in regards to Mr. Kane's possible suitability for parole. It has been with due diligence that this panel has given careful consideration to its decision in this matter, therefore we have decided that the only proper and correct decision is...'

She suddenly stopped talking, leaving everyone in the room to hang on her words, before she finally continued. 'Mr. Kane this panel has found you to be suitable for parole, and we will be submitting your file for review and consideration to the full board, who will have 120 days to make their decision. Should they agree with the findings of this panel, your file will be sent on to the governor's desk for a final review and decision, and he will have up to 30 days in which to make his decision. So, do you understand that your release on parole will not take place until all reviews have been done, and that could take a total of 150 days?' I sat there looking at her for a moment, still in a bit of shock, when I realised she had asked me a question, so I calmly responded, 'Yes, I do understand, and I want to thank the panel.'

She stated that the hearing was now concluded and with that I felt the guard touch my shoulder, and he led me back to the interview room, along with my attorney. It was my attorney who spoke first saying, 'See why I insisted that it would be in your best interest to attend the hearing, even though you had limited participation, it was the fact that, after how the last hearing before went, you still had the ability to face her again. I do believe that the reason we drew her panel was exactly because of how she behaved last time, and the governing body of the BPH wanted her to have an opportunity to correct the errors of her ways. If you had postponed citing her previous behaviour as the reason, it quite frankly may have gone against you at future boards. So all in all, I think you made a good choice for everyone. Good luck, you have been found suitable, my job is done, and I wish you well on your trip back to the UK.' With that, he shook my hand and the guard escorted him to the staff exit, then a few minutes later came back for me.

As the guard let me out of the board area, he said 'Congratulations, second time hopefully will be the charm, I wish you all the best.' Now again walking down the corridor back to my unit L-3, I knew I was running the gauntlet of well-wishers, as the boardroom officers always let the staff know the outcome, so they can be prepared if the inmate takes a decision badly. This time it seemed everyone who wished me well on getting a parole date again were a little more subdued. I did get back to my cell, grabbed my shower gear and after a nice hot shower laid down to get some sleep and start the waiting game again. I was found suitable on August 16th, 2017, and although I had a maximum time to wait of 150 days, you can imagine how shocked I was when on December 17th, 2017, I was called to my counsellor's office and told that I had been approved and was to be handed over to immigration and transferred to a detention centre the following day. As I was only allowed to take one small suitcase with me, I had less than 24 hours in which to say goodbye to those who knew me and to dispose of all the possessions that I had accumulated over the years.

So, there you have it. Hopefully, I have shown you what prison is like, what some of the inmates are like, and for those who are lifers, just how hard it is to be paroled from a Californian prison. I know of many who, admitted, were teenage criminals, but now they are old men, and like most people have matured and grown sensible with age. Yet every board does not see the older man, just the reckless teenager. Perhaps, like me, they are accused of extra crimes they never committed. Still, that is the system that the Californian taxpayer seems to be happy with, as every one of those prisoners is costing them more than $80,000 dollars a year. I leave you to decide whether it is a good system or not.